Preferential Trading Agreements in Asia

Published by Academic Foundation
in association with

Indian Council for Research on
International Economic Relations,
New Delhi

Preferential Trading Agreements in Asia

Towards an Asian Economic Community

Editor

AMITA BATRA

ACADEMIC FOUNDATION

NEW DELHI

First published in 2008
by

ACADEMIC FOUNDATION
4772-73 / 23 Bharat Ram Road, (23 Ansari Road),
Darya Ganj, New Delhi - 110 002 (India).
Phones : 23245001 / 02 / 03 / 04.
Fax : +91-11-23245005.
E-mail : academic@vsnl.com
www. academicfoundation.com

in association with:
Indian Council for Research on International Economic Relations
(ICRIER), New Delhi.
www.icrier.org

Cataloging in Publication Data--DK
Courtesy: D.K. Agencies (P) Ltd. <docinfo@dkagencies.com>

Preferential trading agreements in Asia : towards an Asian economic community / editor, Amita Batra.
p. cm.
Contributed articles.
Includes index.
ISBN 13: 9788171886302
ISBN 10: 8171886302

1. Asia--Commercial treaties. 2. Asia--Economic integration. 3. Association of South East Asian Nations. I. Batra, Amita.

DDC 337.15 22

Typeset by Italics India, New Delhi.
Printed and bound in India.

CONTENTS

List of Tables and Figures

Tables

Figures

About the Editor/Contributors

Editor:

Amita Batra is Associate Professor, South Asian Studies in the School of International Studies, Jawaharlal Nehru University, New Delhi, India. She has worked as Senior Fellow at the Indian Council for Research on International Economic Relations (ICRIER), New Delhi for five years and before that Reader, Economics, in Hindu College, University of Delhi. She has to her credit several national and international publications in refereed and other journals, books etc. As invited speaker Dr. Batra has made presentations at various national and international conferences including a talk at the "World Knowledge Forum" held in Seoul in October, 2006. She was a visiting Fellow at the Crawford School of Economics and Government, Australian National University, Canberra and the Lee Kuan Yew School of Public Policy, Singapore. Dr. Batra has also worked as external consultant for the World Bank's New Delhi Office. Dr. Batra is a Ph.D. in Economics from the Delhi School of Economics, University of Delhi, India.

Contributors:

Ramgopala Agarwala ..... *Consultant, RIS, New Delhi.*

Amita Batra .... *Senior Fellow, Indian Council for Research on International Economic Relations (ICRIER), New Delhi, India. Presently, Associate Professor, School of International Studies, Jawaharlal Nehru University, New Delhi, India.*

Peter Drysdale .... *Professor, The Australian National University, Canberra, Australia.*

Lu Jianren .... *Professor, The Institute of Asia Pacific Studies, Chinese Academy of Social Sciences, Beijing, China.*

Rajiv Kumar .... *Director, Indian Council for Research on International Economic Relations (ICRIER), New Delhi, India.*

Wisarn Pupphavesa ...... *Advisor, Thailand Development Research Institute, Bangkok, Thailand.*

Rahul Sen .... *Fellow, Institute of South East Asian Studies (ISEAS), Singapore.*

Sasatra Sudsawasd .... *Lecturer, National Institute of Development Administration (NIDA), Bangkok, Thailand.*

Preface

Regional economic integration in Asia has gathered momentum over the last decade reflecting several factors. The Asian financial crisis along with other developments like the demonstration effect of institution building outside the region, notably the continent—wide trade blocs in the North—i.e. the EU and the NAFTA, growing concern about discrimination caused by preferential trade agreements in the rest of the world, relatively slow progress in the multilateral fora and the rise of India and China as two of the world's most dynamic economies have helped underscore not just the interdependence among countries in the region but also highlighted the significance of a regional cooperation mechanism to promote deeper integration as also effectively deal with the common challenges of globalisation.

In spite of these developments the path to regional economic cooperation in Asia is not straightforward. There is the lack of cohesiveness in the region in terms of developmental stages of member nations, political systems as well as the centrifugal force of historical antagonism and political rivalries. There is however a strong economic rationale to building an effective regional institutional framework for cooperation. East Asian economies have an incentive to reduce transaction costs and promote the *de facto* integration so as to facilitate the dense vertical intra-industry trade linkages among these economies. India with its increasingly evident complementarities in manufacturing and services with East Asian economies is becoming part of the East Asia trade and investment nexus.

In its search for a regional identity the region has thus far grappled with several proposals like the ASEAN plus three (APT), the plus three etc. More recently the East Asia Summit (EAS) has emerged as an open and more inclusive forum to promote a full fledged east Asian community that may then become the harbinger of the Asian economic community (AEC). How the EAS will lead to an AEC is yet not known. Several aspects pertaining to ASEAN integration and harmonisation of the Asian noodle bowl of trade agreements need to be resolved.

It is against this background that ICRIER with the aid of a grant from the International Development Research Centre, Ottawa, Canada, organised an international workshop on "Preferential Trading Agreements in Asia: Towards an Asian Economic Community" in March 2006. This book which is a collection of the papers presented at the workshop will go a long way in disseminating insights of the regional experts on the concept of economic integration in Asia to a wider audience. The book will also, it is felt, contribute to a better understanding of the challenges and complexities associated with deeper integration in Asia and thereby help shape the policymaker's vision of a more integrated Asia.

Rajiv Kumar
Director
ICRIER, New Delhi

1

Introduction

AMITA BATRA

In Asia today, there is a fundamental rethinking on the strategic assumptions that influence the emergence of regional economic architecture. Several factors have contributed to this development; predominant among these are—the end of cold war, liberalisation, economic reform and the consequent convergence of economic policies among Asian economies. Further, the emergence of continent-wide preferential trading arrangements (PTAs) in the North like the European Union (EU) and North American Free Trade Agreement (NAFTA) has meant that over 60 per cent of world trade takes place on a preferential basis. As a result, the growing concern about discrimination and fear of isolation has given momentum to the efforts towards evolving an institutional mechanism for regional economic integration in Asia. This response has also been conditioned by the desire for a regional identity owing to a shared vulnerability to economic and non-economic transnational threats arising out of disasters such as the financial meltdown of 1997, terrorist attacks on Bali and elsewhere in the region, Severe Acute Respiratory Syndrome (SARS) and the Indian Ocean *tsunami*. Several configurations have consequently been proposed in the region like the ASEAN Plus Three (APT), along with the bilateral initiatives between member economies of the Association of Southeast Asian Nations (ASEAN) and Northeast Asia.

Notwithstanding these developments, the process of regional cooperation in East Asia is yet not well-defined and the search for an institutional identity continues. While proposals like the ASEAN+3 have been logical outcomes of the trade led market integration that the region has experienced over the last couple of decades, it is the rise of India and its likely influence along with China on the economic landscape of the region that has forced reconsideration of the existing institutional configurations. Hence, attempts at the establishment of an institutional identity thus far restricted to the 'ASEAN+ Three' and the creation of an East Asian Community have been more recently extended to a more inclusive East Asia Summit (EAS) process.

At the First East Asia Summit which was held in December 2005 in Kuala Lumpur, Malaysia, 16 nations, that is, the ASEAN+3 (China, Japan, South Korea) +3 (Australia, New Zealand and India) recognising the increasing interlinkages and growing interdependence agreed to deepen integration and cooperation in order to promote the creation of a harmonious and prosperous community of nations. At the Summit, ASEAN was accepted as the driving force of the Asian partnership. The Agreement at the East Asia Summit also reiterated that it should remain open and outward looking. In this context, the Russian Federation's expression of interest to participate in the East Asia Summit was welcomed and it was agreed to consider its participation in future East Asia Summits based on the criteria established by ASEAN. The East Asia Summit has since emerged as an integral component of the evolving regional architecture. It is believed that the EAS together with the ASEAN+3 and the ASEAN+1 processes could play a significant role in building the Asian economic community. In this process of an evolving Asian regional economic architecture, some of the issues that need to be highlighted and focused upon are briefly discussed below while having been dealt with in greater detail in the various chapters of the book.

The plan of the book with a brief outline of each chapter follows.

Economic integration under the ASEAN+3: First proposed at the 2000 Singapore ASEAN Summit, the driving force of this configuration is the region's desire to evolve an effective mechanism of cooperation to facilitate and strengthen the *de facto* market-led integration evident in the dense business networks of vertical intra-industry trade in East Asia. There is at present no formal agreement binding the 13 economies of this configuration. Nevertheless, of late it has been perceived as the most appropriate forum for management of regional economic integration. Notwithstanding the diversity in economic and trade strengths of member nations, the forum has to its credit members who are bound through their dependence on intra-regional trade as a means to enhance their external competitiveness and a track record of financial cooperation. The forum in its present form also allows for expansion beyond the existing membership.

The ASEAN+1 processes: Triggered by the China–ASEAN initiative several plurilateral initiatives are underway in the region. In November 2002, ASEAN and China signed a framework agreement (FA) on comprehensive economic cooperation. This provides for an ASEAN–China Free Trade Area (ACFTA) by 2010 for the more developed ASEAN-6 and by 2015 for the Cambodia, Laos, Myanmar and Vietnam (CLMV) countries. The ACFTA had a domino effect on excluded East Asian economies. Reactionary trade agreements with ASEAN were initiated so as to address possible trade discrimination on account of the ACFTA. A closer economic partnership agreement has been signed between ASEAN and Australia and New Zealand (ASEAN-CER). In 2005, ASEAN began negotiating an FTA with those nations. In 2002-2003, ASEAN and Japan established the ASEAN–Japan Comprehensive Economic Partnership. This included elements of a possible free trade area and is to be implemented by 2012 (2017 for newer ASEAN members). ASEAN signed a FW Agreement for an FTA with India in 2003. With South Korea, ASEAN decided to start negotiations for an FTA in 2004. An ASEAN–Korea FTA pact that covers only trade in goods was signed in 2006. It is important in this context to state that even though ASEAN may negotiate an FTA Agreement, it is to be implemented as if it is a bilateral agreement as ASEAN is not a common market itself. This in fact also implies that each ASEAN member is free to pursue bilateral FTAs on its own. Singapore has been the most active ASEAN member country to do so.

Intersecting bilateral and plurilateral agreements: The ACFTA-triggered domino effect has not only generated plurilateral ASEAN 10 agreements in the region but also led to the emergence of several bilateral deals initially among the excluded nations (Japan–Korea) followed by the ASEAN member nations. Triggered by Japan and Korea the trend for bilateral FTAs strengthened rapidly as this route seemed to be a more easily negotiable and practical vehicle for liberalisation. Singapore's move out of the ASEAN 10 to forge its own FTA deals stimulated other members to explore FTAs collectively and individually, with other countries. As a consequence a multilayered approach to regionalism in Asia appears to have emerged—there is the intra-East Asia (Japan–Singapore), intra-Western Pacific (such as Singapore–New Zealand), combined with the regional configurations like the ASEAN+3 and the plurilaterals like ASEAN–CER, ASEAN–China, ASEAN–Korea and ASEAN–India.

This system of overlapping layers with extensive interlinkages implies not just additional operational costs but also lends an element of fragility to regionalism in Asia. An important step that the region therefore, needs to take is consolidation of the various trade agreements in Asia. In fact, making various sub-regional initiatives into region-wide (and even inter-regional) cooperation agreements which are as inclusive as possible would also maximise the potential for creating greater trade and investment opportunities.

Expansion of the ASEAN+3 and amalgamation of the ASEAN+1 FTAs are two possible options for consolidation. ASEAN+3, for reasons stated earlier, is an ongoing and credible initiative. The ASEAN+1s on the other hand are either being negotiated or yet to be implemented initiatives. The harmonisation of these initiatives is therefore, a practical possibility. In this context, the institutional advance in the form of the 'open and outward looking' East Asia Summit needs to be pursued with greater seriousness.

The ASEAN-centric regional architecture: An important aspect that derives from the above discussion is that no matter what the chosen path towards economic integration in Asia the central place that ASEAN has come to occupy in the process cannot be denied. As regional economic integration in Asia is ASEAN-centric, its feasibility to a large extent will depend upon the progress of ASEAN's internal integration. It is thus important that the ASEAN evolve as a single market and not continue to be an association of 10 diverse nations. ASEAN has put in place building blocs towards achieving an integrated ASEAN market. These include the AFTA (ASEAN Free Trade Area 1992) and its main tool, the Common Effective Preferential Tariff Scheme and initiatives for deeper integration—the AIA (ASEAN Investment Area 1998) and the AFAS (ASEAN Framework Agreement on Services 1995). The progress so far has however been limited. A lot more needs to be done to propel integrative forces in trade in goods as also in investment and services liberalisation. An essential feature of the agenda for accelerating ASEAN integration is institutional change. The ASEAN decision making process has to steer away from consensus based decision making and accommodation of the lowest common denominator to a more formal rule based decision making mechanism.

Financial cooperation: A final issue in the context of Asian economic integration relates to financial cooperation. In the post-East Asian financial crisis period there is a growing realisation for the need to promote financial stability in the region. Asian countries have made noteworthy achievements in post-crisis initiatives in financial cooperation. In particular, in May 2000, the ASEAN+3 finance ministers agreed to what is called the "Chiang Mai Initiative (CMI)." The initiative aims at providing support to participating ASEAN+3 countries in times of financial/currency crises by creating a network of bilateral swap arrangements for short-term liquidity needs. This bilateral swap arrangement has been formalised among China, Indonesia, Japan, Korea, Malaysia, the Philippines, Singapore and Thailand, the countries of ASEAN+3. The ASEAN+3 countries have also recently announced their possible move toward 'multilateralisation' of the current bilateral swap arrangement under the CMI by pooling their reserves to address its inherent shortcomings of funding uncertainty and inefficiency. Other initiatives include enhanced information exchange and policy dialogue, and regional capital market development. While contributing to crisis prevention and management these reforms may also assist in management of high savings of the region and provision of opportunities so that more of Asia's savings remain in the region. Wider investment of available savings in the region is at present limited possibly owing to the as yet underdeveloped market infrastructure and investor concerns about efficient pricing and liquidity and perceived weaknesses in legal certainty and in regulatory frameworks. Steps to create regional Asian financial markets, such as the Asian Bond Market Initiative (ABMI), the Asian Bond Fund (ABF), increased links between stock exchanges, and the ASEAN Finance Roadmap and efforts to collaborate in adopting global standards and best practices could go a long way in resolving these issues.

The above issues are discussed in diverse ways in the ensuing chapters of this book. Chapters 2, 3 and 4 together offer a conceptual treatment of regional economic integration in Asia. Chapter 2 is an Asia-Pacific perspective while the following two chapters provide the perspectives from India and China—the two economies that could reshape the existing visions of Asian economic integration. Chapters 5, 6 and 7 discuss issues of deeper economic integration. Chapter 5 discusses the inevitable need to resolve the noodle bowl of bilateral and plurilateral deals for successful Asian integration. Chapters 6 and 7 deal with specific issues of liberalisation of services and investment in ASEAN and regional financial cooperation respectively. A brief outline of each chapter is given below.

About the Book

Chapter 2 "The Concept of the Asian Economic Community" authored by Peter Drysdale discusses the development of Asia-Pacific economic arrangements and the principle of 'open regionalism'. The history of the East Asian and Pacific economies and polities, the structure of the regional economy, and regional political imperatives, Drysdale explains, have driven regional arrangements that involve no overarching supranational structures or a predominant role of any one government. He further elaborates on how unilateral liberalisation was to be the driving force for international integration in this region. Moving then to the emerging scenario in East Asia and across the Pacific, Drysdale states that the only way to integrate the set of competing but separate preferential or discriminatory trade arrangements is by means of the framework of a comprehensive round of multilateral negotiations in the WTO. As for India, Drysdale highlights the evolving perspective of its place in the emerging global economy and the tremendous potential for creating synergies with East Asia. A re-positioning of strategic significance has occurred and this has opened up ideas about the value of more comprehensive economic and other cooperation with East Asia and the concept of an Asian Economic Community (AEC) in which India might play a leading role. For India to be successful the chapter recommends that the focus on a global strategy is imperative. Further with respect to Asian economic integration key instruments would remain as the ASEAN, Asia Pacific Economic Cooperation (APEC) and, now to a lesser extent, ASEAN+3. According to Drysdale even though India's participation in the East Asian Summit is symbolic, East Asian regionalism itself is more likely, if it happens, under the broader framework of the APEC. This would not only ensure continuing US engagement in the region but also India's inclusion as an economic partner rather than an instrument of political strategy.

Amita Batra in the following chapter entitled "Preferential Trading Agreements in Asia: Towards an Asian Economic Community" explains the economic rationale and potential of an ASEAN+3+1 regional trade arrangement in Asia. Using the evidence on intra-bloc trends in trade, trade intensity and potential for trade creation, Batra establishes the economic strength of the proposed bloc as a strong contender for regional economic integration and provides the justification for the westward extension of ASEAN to include India. The chapter identifies the most efficient approach to such a formation. Two approaches, one, with India as the last entrant to a prior ASEAN+3 formation and two, a convergence of independent ASEAN+1 FTAs by the Plus Four economies are examined. The conclusion is drawn in favour of the convergence of ASEAN+1 FTAs. The consequent costs in terms of both trade diversion and first mover advantage have been evaluated. The scope for trade diversion under this arrangement is shown to be almost negligible. The cost of late entry *vis-a-vis* China is highest for India and sectors where India may be adversely affected on account of the ASEAN–China FTA and the Early Harvest Programme (EHP) are identified in the chapter. For a successful convergence of the four ASEAN+1 FTAs the author recommends that these agreements be harmonised. The fact that these initiatives are still under negotiation will be a facilitating factor in this context the author concludes.

Lu Jianren in Chapter 4 presents the Chinese view on Asian Economic Integration. In the current context of economic integration in Asia, the author discusses four interconnected mechanisms of regional cooperation and integration that have formed in East Asia: ASEAN, ASEAN+1 (ASEAN–China, ASEAN–Japan, ASEAN–Korea),

China–Japan–Korea, and ASEAN+3 even while the last one has emerged as the main channel. Jianren in this chapter also highlights the gradual convergence of East Asia and South Asia in the context of emerging economic integration initiatives in South, Central and West Asia. The chapter also discusses the different strategies followed by the most active proponents of the Asian economic integration that is, ASEAN, China, Japan, Korea and India. These are: the 'concentric strategy' of ASEAN, 'big periphery' of China, 'expanded Asian community concept' of Japan, Korea's proposal identifying the North east as the hub and India's proposition of the ASEAN+3+1 as the predecessor to Asian economic integration. Jianren concludes his analysis by calling the EAS combination the blueprint of a mutually beneficial Pan-Asian Economic Community.

Rahul Sen in Chapter 5 discusses the Bilateral Trade and Economic Cooperation Agreements (BTAs) in ASEAN and their implications for Asian Economic Integration. In a conservative estimate Sen states that if the proposed and currently negotiated BTAs do come into force and their preferences are effectively utilised, nearly half or more of ASEAN and India's merchandise trade is going to be driven by 'new regionalism', while such BTAs would cover about a quarter or more of China's total merchandise trade. The chapter undertakes analysis of the benefits of BTAs in terms of accelerating the pace of multilateral liberalisation, initiating policy reforms in areas like services that may be hard to achieve under the multilateral process, and as being perceived as a positive signal towards enhancing economic and strategic cooperation, and addressing regional security concerns as also concerns such as the potential for trade diversion away from the spokes towards the emerging hub of these BTAs, the complexity and consequent costs of the overlapping BTAs, underutilisation of BTAs alongside inefficient use of scarce negotiating resources. As the concerns are likely to outweigh the benefits, Sen in this chapter argues that in their present form the BTAs are more in the nature of stumbling blocks. In this context therefore, Sen proposes that the option of Pan-Asian economic integration is better as it would facilitate the exploitation of complementarities among the Asian economies to create synergies for mutual benefit. India's role is crucial, as it shares significant complementarities with East Asian economies. However, the author sounds a caveat in that ASEAN needs to have a clear and comprehensive blueprint for economic integration and the current pace of progress of AIA and AFAS and the nature of existing/under negotiation BTAs may not provide the best inputs for this blueprint.

In Chapter 6, Wisarn Pupphavesa and Sasastra Sudswasd outline the objectives of the ASEAN Investment Area (AIA) highlighting the provision of preferential differential treatment for less developed new members of ASEAN in the agreement. Discussing the progress of the AIA process Pupphavesa highlights the significance of the ASEAN Framework Agreement for the Integration of Priority Sectors signed in 2004 to accelerate the integration of priority sectors in realising the end goal of ASEAN Economic Community by 2020. As regards the ASEAN Framework Agreement for Services (AFAS) which is intended to improve the efficiency and competitiveness of ASEAN services suppliers through elimination of restriction to trade in services and improvements in market access and ensuring national treatment for services suppliers among ASEAN countries in all four modes of services supply, Pupphavesa argues that the commitments of liberalisation are consistent with, but beyond member countries' commitment under GATS. The AFAS is therefore, a GATS-Plus Agreement. Using a modified gravity model and data covering FDI outflows from 30 Organization for Economic Cooperation and Development (OECD) countries to 59 OECD and non-OECD countries over the period 1980–2003, Wisarn shows that an increase in the proportion of FDI receipts to GDP of ASEAN+5 significantly increases other recipients' ratio as well.

In the last chapter Ramgopal Agarwala and Rajiv Kumar question the relevance of a PTA (Plurilateral Trade Agreement) in Asia given the slow growth of trade in the region. The chapter makes the proposition that if the US begins to see regional cooperation in Asia as an opportunity for correcting its current account imbalances, it can give a big boost to regional cooperation in Asia. In this context, the authors identify three areas of action; concerted exchange rate policy in Asia for facilitating devaluation of US $ in relation to Asian currencies; regional trade facilitation measures to increase intra-regional trade and increased infrastructure investment to cure 'investment drought' in Asia. For greater impact on the US trade deficits and for minimising intra-Asian trade distortions, a concerted exchange rate management policy and creation of a common currency unit in Asia is proposed in the nature of the IMF's Special Drawing Rights (SDR) that will act as the third reserve currency apart from the Euro and Dollar.

2

Regionalism in Asia and the Pacific

An Asian Economic Community

PETER DRYSDALE

Introduction

The establishment of regional arrangements in East Asia and the Pacific was chiefly a response to the rise of Japan's economic power and the need to include Japan in a framework for managing the growth of regional economic interdependence.

The growth and deepening integration of the East Asian economy was driven by three huge waves of trade and industrial transformation. The first came with the rise of Japan and its emergence as a major industrial power, especially in the first three decades after the Pacific War. The second was led by the newly industrialising economies (NIEs) of Northeast and Southeast Asia in the late 1970s and 1980s. Now there is a third great wave sweeping the region, with the remarkable rise of China. There is also the prospect of a fourth in India. These successive waves of trade and industrial transformation have created a new centre of East Asian economic power that has begun to rival North America and Europe in terms of its contribution to world output and world trade (Drysdale and Terada, 2006). They are at the base of strategies that have shaped the evolution of regional arrangements thus far and will shape their evolution in the future.

These developments, the origins of which date back to Japan's commitment to modernisation in the latter part of the nineteenth century and through the turmoil of accommodating that development in the first half of the twentieth century, proceeded on a smoother course after the Pacific War. Importantly, this was because of the supportive framework provided by the international institutions (such as the GATT, now the WTO, and the IMF) established under the leadership of the United States in the post-War world (Drysdale, 1988). This fact of history is an important reference point in thinking about what India's substantial economic, as opposed to more narrowly diplomatic, interests might be in participation in Asian economic cooperation arrangements.

Recovery and reconstruction in Europe saw the emergence of a united Europe and the Atlantic Alliance framework. There was no similar or easy political or economic solution on offer in East Asia and the Pacific to the rise of post-War Japan and its newly industrialising neighbours. Japan's political position in its neighbourhood was very different (Ohira, 1980; Pacific Community Seminar, 1981; Bonner, 1996). China was a target of hostility but not the same target of mutual hostility as the Soviet Union, especially after the Nixon-Zhou accord of 1971. America's military-security relations with others in the neighbourhood were very different. The economic, political, societal and institutional conditions in the neighbourhood were extremely diverse (Soesastro, 1994). Furthermore, the regional economy was in continuing and large-scale transformation. The problem was how to accommodate the rise of Japan in a framework of international economic pluralism (Drysdale, 1988). India had not yet committed to openness and reform and was not part of the process of growing regional economic interdependence.

This paper traces the development of Asia Pacific economic arrangements and how they were founded on the principle of 'open regionalism'. It describes the nature and purpose of APEC (Asia Pacific Economic Cooperation) and the challenges to APEC in the late 1990s. It traces the emergence of East Asian regionalism as a competitor for political and diplomatic attention. It highlights the growing engagement of India with East Asia, reviews the future agenda for regional cooperation and the prospects for an Asian Economic Community (AEC) in the near future.

Regionalism in East Asia and the Pacific

The idea of APEC was the solution to the problem of the rise of Japan in its political-economic dimension (Drysdale 1988; Terada, 1999). The hub and spokes military-security alliances remained in place between Washington and East Asian and Western Pacific capitals. Though they comprehend less and less adequately the realities of China's political reach in the region, they remain in place and were given, at least temporarily, extended life and invigoration by the circumstances that followed September 11.

This was the context in which Australia and Japan together played such an important role in articulating the regional idea in Asia and the Pacific and in the work that led to the formation of APEC.

A huge, strategic resource and energy trade relationship developed between Japan and Australia after the normalisation of the relationship between the two countries through the Agreement on Commerce in 1957. This completed the first element of the economic and political triangle that was to develop between North America, Japan and the other economies of East Asia (including the Western Pacific) over subsequent decades. The political-security arrangements between the United States and Japan and the United States and Australia, separately, for example, provided an implicit, if not explicit, framework of political confidence within which the Australia-Japan relationship came to grow and flourish (Drysdale, 1988).

By the late 1960s and during the 1970s the growing web of East Asian and Western Pacific interdependence required a different role for Japan in regional (and global) affairs, a role that acknowledged the economic and potential political influence of Japan, beyond the bilateral relationship with the United States (Drysdale and Patrick, 1979). This was the focus of policy innovation in regional diplomacy over the two decades or so before APEC was launched in 1989. The intellectual, business and governmental dialogues around the region over those years eventually delivered a regional inter-governmental arrangement in the form of APEC, an organisation that was uniquely designed to suit the particular political and economic situation of East Asia and the Pacific (Soesastro, 1994). It was designed to promote common policy priorities that were being articulated within the market economies of the region and to support national domestic efforts at liberalisation and economic reform.

Meanwhile, in the 1970s and 1980s, the second great wave of industrialisation in Northeast and Southeast Asia gathered strength.

The newly industrialising economies of Northeast and Southeast Asia developed intense trading relations within the region with Japan and across the Pacific with America. A growing feature of regional economic interdependence was the role played by direct foreign investment. The growth of these East Asian economies saw them take over Japan's share in world markets for labour-intensive goods, such as textiles and clothing and, later, even consumer electronics (Drysdale, 2005b). Japan took production capacity offshore into the region and North American and European investors also established production networks in East Asia. China has since become an important investment destination and international production centre.

In its initial years APEC's focus was on accommodating the rise of Japan and her new regional role. However, the history of the East Asian and Pacific economies and polities, the structure of the regional economy and regional political imperatives recommended regional arrangements in which no one country played the central role (Drysdale, 1988; Drysdale and Elek, 1997). APEC also recommended a set of inter-governmental relationships that involved no overarching supranational structures. And it encouraged a regional agenda that embodied significantly global objectives.

Unlike other regional arrangements, within Europe or North America, APEC eschewed inward-looking approaches to regional economic integration, focusing instead on the region's powerful global trade and economic interests, initially through pressing a successful conclusion to the Uruguay Round of trade negotiations in the GATT. The organising idea of APEC was 'open regionalism' or the promotion of trade liberalisation on a 'most favoured nation' or non-discriminatory basis (Yamazawa, 1992; Garnaut, 1996). But open regionalism had a political and diplomatic dimension as well as a trade and economic dimension. After successfully exercising some leverage over Europe in these multilateral negotiations through its first Leaders' Summit in Seattle in 1993, APEC sought to operationalise the idea of open regionalism beyond its role as a regional coalition in the global arena (APEC, 1993; Drysdale and Garnaut, 1993; Bergsten, 1994). It specifically left open the inclusion of other countries such as India and, in its core conception, deliberately sought to avoid discrimination against newcomers, such as India, to the process of outward-looking growth (Drysdale and Garnaut, 1993). The Bogor Declaration, from the APEC Summit in Indonesia in 1994, was a bold and innovative step which set a transition path to trade and investment liberalisation for APEC members.

The 1980s and early 1990s saw strong commitment in East Asia and Australasia to unilateral trade liberalisation and internationally-oriented economic reform. These policy developments were the driving force behind exceptionally strong regional trade and economic growth, and the emergence of the East Asian hemisphere as a new pole of growth and influence in the world economy (Garnaut, 1996). They remain at the heart of the APEC agenda. The Bogor goals defined a new path towards an open trade and investment regime in East Asia and the Pacific, setting, 2010 and 2020, respectively, as the targets for trade and investment liberalisation, for the developed and the developing countries of the region (APEC, 1994).

While APEC is unlikely to be able to declare complete victory on trade and investment liberalisation by these target dates, there has been sufficient progress towards the goals to justify the new mode that it set in place for encouraging economic reform. China's use of APEC as a vehicle for liberalisation and reform on the way to accession to the WTO is a notable example of APEC's success in promoting open trade via this strategy (APEC, 1995).

Border protection, of course, is not the only, nor probably the most important, barrier to deeper economic integration. Contingent protection remains an important issue. Behind-the-border liberalisation and reform (APEC's trade and investment facilitation agenda) offer a far bigger future prospect for economic gain. I shall return to this aspect of APEC's future agenda below.

The approach to cooperation within Asia Pacific economic institutions involved no legally binding institutional arrangements. Rather it made a virtue of the necessity that diversity of political and diplomatic circumstance prevented aping European and North American regional institutions, stressing capacity building and transition towards policy goals by independent, but mutually reinforcing, commitment and not by negotiated agreement or fiat. This suited a region in which newly won independence and sovereignty were jealously guarded, where there was immense political, cultural and institutional diversity and in which political ownership was a priority (Garnaut, 2000; Harris, 2000; Drysdale and Terada, 2006).

East Asian Regionalism and Bilateralism

The East Asian financial crisis and the failure of both global financial institutions and global trading institutions to maintain financial stability in the region and the momentum of growth through multilateral trade liberalisation presented a major challenge to APEC's economic agenda in the late 1990s (Harris, 2000; Wesley, 2001). The difficulty in dealing with the 'hard' issues of liberalisation on the basis of volunteerism coincided with the erosion of confidence in global solutions and in Washington's commitment to global solutions. These were the circumstances that spawned the emergence of a new regionalism in East Asia.

These circumstances appeared quite different from those that encouraged the development of APEC, built on the principles of open regionalism. This was not only a product of East Asia's complex political response to Washington's role in the 1997 financial crisis. There was also loss of faith in APEC's capacity to deal with the problems of the time as also in global arrangements like the IMF and the WTO. There was intensification of preferential trading initiatives elsewhere, including in North America, in contradistinction to the principles to which APEC had in the past adhered. And there was disappointment in the failure to launch a new WTO round of trade negotiations in Seattle, which was central to the success of APEC's trade liberalisation agenda (Drysdale, 2005a and 2005b; MacIntyre and Soesastro, 2005). All these developments were used to justify the heading off in a new direction to establish ASEAN+3 and to negotiate preferential trade arrangements in East Asia at the end of the twentieth century.

By one measure, the rise of East Asia in the world economy still has a long way to go. When national products are valued at current exchange rates, the United States economy, accounting for more than 30 per cent of world output, appears resurgent against a flagging East Asian challenge. East Asia's share of world output declined from around 25 per cent at its peak in the mid-1990s to 20 per cent in 2002.

Moreover, Japan—by this measure, still the second biggest economy in the world—appears to dominate the East Asian economy, accounting for roughly two-thirds of the region's total output.

But this is only one measure of the relative importance of East Asia in the world economy, and probably not the most accurate, because of the way in which current exchange rates and short-term influences upon them distort the underlying picture. A better measure uses purchasing power parity (PPP) valuations of national product to estimate the relative size of economies in the global economy. East Asia's share of world output, by this measure, has risen substantially over the past two decades from just over 15 per cent in 1980 to over 27 per cent in 2004, having overtaken the United States by 1993. Moreover, within East Asia, China's share of world output had already surpassed that of Japan by 1994 and, by 2004, its share of world output was already more than half that of the United States. China's economy, of course, remains less sophisticated than that of Japan, but its sheer scale now gives it much larger weight in world output. While East Asia's share of world trade has not grown so strongly in the last decade, at almost a quarter of world trade it more than matches that of North America. Measured in PPP terms, India still only accounts for just under 6 per cent of world output, less than half the size of China and much smaller if income is valued at current exchange rates. Within East Asia, the story is one of rising trade share for China and steadily falling trade share for Japan (China's share of world trade, measured appropriately as China's trade plus the trade of Hong Kong net of intra-China–Hong Kong trade, is already over 7 per cent). While India's share of world trade is growing, it still lags well behind China and other countries in East Asia.

This is the reality of the recent rise of the East Asian economy and the growing weight of China within it, driven by the third wave of East Asian trade and industrial transformation. It was at the base of the growing support for the idea of East Asian cooperation arrangements. But it also underlines the value of a broader regional framework, such as APEC, within which to manage the economic and political process of adjustment to the change and to support outward-looking development strategies.

The emergence of ASEAN+3 and the idea of an East Asian economic community reflected the interest in re-grouping and building a framework for substantive economic cooperation within the East Asian region (Drysdale and Terada, 2006). ASEAN+3 was not established as a regional trading arrangement. It was set up in response to the financial crisis, to foster East Asian cooperation in financial affairs and project East Asian interests globally. An overarching objective was to provide a framework for demonstrating East Asian influence and leadership on regional and international affairs. The initial focus was very much on regional financial cooperation but that was simply the point from which to promote high level economic and political dialogue (Soesastro, 2001).

In January 2002 in Singapore, Prime Minister Koizumi proposed an East Asian Community encompassing cooperation beyond trade and financial issues (and including Australia and New Zealand) to promote regional integration. The agenda of ASEAN+3 extends beyond the issue of financial cooperation and the ambition, stated more clearly at meetings in Bali in 2005, is for the evolution of an East Asian Economic Community.

A parallel development was the rush towards bilateral or sub-regional free trade agreements (FTAs). These are preferential or discriminatory trade arrangements. Preferential trade arrangements within East Asia (including the participation of key regional economies such as Japan, China and South Korea) had never before found favour. It was thought that not only would they inflict costs on important economic partners, but they were also likely to elevate political tensions in predictable ways between countries that were included and those that were excluded from such arrangements. This was acknowledged explicitly while designing the architecture for APEC. Yet in the early 21st century there has been a rash of new proposals and initiatives in East Asia to promote bilateral FTAs of an explicitly discriminatory kind.

Within the region, the Japan-Singapore Agreement has already been signed. Singapore has also signed agreements with Australia and the United States. The first significant proposal was for an FTA between Japan and Korea at the time of President Kim Dae-jung's historic visit to Japan in 1998. Japan–Korea, Japan–Singapore (concluded in January

2002), Japan–Mexico, China–ASEAN, Korea–Chile, Japan–ASEAN, Thailand–Australia, Singapore–New Zealand, Korea–ASEAN, US–ASEAN, CER–ASEAN, Japan–Korea–China or Taiwan are some of the arrangements that have been concluded, mooted or are on the slipways. The United States has recently committed to negotiating an FTA with Korea. Except for the China–ASEAN proposal, the negotiation of arrangements with ASEAN countries has so far proceeded bilaterally rather than with ASEAN collectively.

India is now joining in this process with East Asia through the negotiation of arrangements with ASEAN. India was less allergic to discriminatory trade strategies, partly because until recently global market access had a low priority and there were ambitions to promote economic and political cooperation in the subcontinent through an FTA within SAARC. I shall return to these issues below.

At the centre of this shift in policy direction was Japan (Munakata, 2001). Japan was then the only major economy in the world other than China or Korea that was not a member of any FTA or economic union. One of the consequences of Japan's FTA initiatives was to encourage China to join the FTA game. Most importantly, China was freed to propose an FTA with ASEAN for dealing with the political sensitivities about its economic rise in Southeast Asia. The reaction in Australia was also of consequence. Advised that a comprehensive FTA was not possible with Japan because of agriculture, Australia's initial reaction was to try to secure an arrangement between CER and ASEAN. Rebuffed initially in that bid, Australia, significantly, scrambled to negotiate an FTA with the United States and sought to do deals with Singapore and Thailand (both of which have been signed) (Drysdale, 2005b). Australia has now entered into negotiations with ASEAN and is the first developed country after New Zealand to commit to the negotiation of an FTA with China.

What is emerging in East Asia and across the Pacific is a set of competing but separate preferential or discriminatory trade arrangements, ordered around the power and leverage of the large economies, in negotiating bilateral trade deals. China, the United States and Japan are the hubs in this process. Korea has similar aspirations. Other countries are the spokes around one or the other or all three of these hubs. It is difficult for such a system of hubs and spokes to link up except within the framework of a comprehensive round of multilateral negotiations in the WTO. But even then, once established, these preferential arrangements are difficult to unravel because they protect producers within them from third party competition and those producers have a vested interest in not giving away their preferred position (Findlay, 2002).

In East Asia, the principal FTA contest is between China and Japan. The structure of this contest can be seen in the pattern of FTA deals already completed or under negotiation within the region. Across the Pacific, the United States has embarked on its own hub and spokes strategy (Drysdale, 2005b).

India and Engagement with East Asia

At the very beginning of its outward-looking economic reforms, India committed to a 'Look East' strategy. This symbolised the interest in emulating the performance and learning from the experience of its East Asian neighbours. Success in boosting economic growth and deepening specialisation inevitably led to closer trade and investment ties with East Asian economies, especially with Southeast Asia and increasingly with China and Northeast Asia.

India has sought to deepen its economic relations with East Asian economies through a wide range of initiatives in bilateral and regional economic diplomacy. India became a sectoral dialogue partner with ASEAN in 1992, seeking to enhance cooperation in trade, investment, tourism, science and technology, and a full dialogue partner at the ASEAN Summit in Bangkok in 1995. An important milestone was the hosting of the first ASEAN-India Leaders Summit in Phnom Penh in 2002. India signed an FTA with Thailand in 2003 and the two countries are working on an Investment Cooperation Agreement (ICA). In 2005, a Comprehensive Economic Cooperation Agreement (CECA) was signed with Singapore. India is considering FTAs with China, Japan and Korea and has an FTA in place with Sri Lanka. A Framework Agreement on establishing an FTA with ASEAN has been signed, although there are many issues to be resolved before it will come to fruition. The Indian approach to rules of origin, for example, is inconsistent with that of ASEAN and will limit the trade creating value of an agreement. Sub-regional cooperation between India and some ASEAN members, including Vietnam, Thailand, Myanmar and Laos, has also been accelerated in ways that are viewed as consistent with strengthening ties with ASEAN and East Asia as a whole.[1] At a strategic level, India, together with Australia and New Zealand, was invited to join the first East Asian Summit in Kuala Lumpur in December 2005. There the Indian leadership focused publicly on the potential development of an Asian Economic Community.

Indeed, the last few years has seen robust growth in India's trade with East Asia, albeit from a relatively low base. The East Asian share of India's exports is between 21 and 31 per cent and imports between 19 and 27 per cent, depending on the data source used to calculate these shares, although the Indian share in East Asian exports and imports is only around 1.2 per cent. India's share in ASEAN exports is higher, at 2.3 per cent (see Table 2.1).[2] Direct foreign investment flows are growing both ways. India's share in world exports has been rising steadily from around 0.7 per cent in the early 1990s to just under 1 per cent in 2004 in the case of exports and from around 0.7 per cent to 1.3 per cent for the same years in the case of imports.[3] And these data do not reflect India's growing role in trade in international services, a role which also has a growing regional dimension. What is less clear is whether these trends have much to do with the specific regional or bilateral initiatives in economic diplomacy that have been put in place or mooted. A more important driver of closer ties with India's fast growing neighbours in East Asia and India's global trade is the process of general trade reform and liberalisation to which India has committed and the access that reform-driven growth in East Asia has provided in these markets. There is still much to be done to capture these gains. Indian tariffs on average remain very high—around three times as high as those in

---

1. These include the Mekong-Ganga Cooperation (MGC) initiative and the Bay of Bengal Initiative for Multilateral and Technical Cooperation (BIMST-EC).

2. Fiscal year data for 2004-05 from India's Ministry of Commerce suggest a share at the lower end of this range while UN Comtrade data suggest a figure at the higher end for calendar year 2004. Data for India's share of East Asian imports are derived from UN Comtrade for 2004.

3. Data for India's shares of world trade are derived from UN Comtrade.

ASEAN, for example—and limit the opportunity for broadly-based trade-oriented growth in labour-using manufacturing industries.

Table 2.1

India: Geographic Structure of Trade, 2004

(Per Cent)

	Export	*Import*	*Total*
USA	7.63	15.18	11.98
Japan	3.81	2.41	3.01
China	7.43	7.09	7.24
Korea	4.55	1.71	2.91
ASEAN	11.78	5.04	7.90
East Asia	30.45	19.73	24.28
EU	25.16	18.53	21.34
Australia	0.86	3.28	2.25
Rest of World	35.90	43.27	40.14

Source: United Nations Comtrade Database.

However, what is important about these developments is that they reflect a major shift in thinking about "India's evolving perspective of the world and its place in the emerging global economy..." and India's growing confidence in "...the tremendous potential for creating synergies in the South-east Asian region" (Chidambaram, 2006). This is a repositioning of strategic significance. It has opened up ideas about the value of more comprehensive economic and other cooperation with East Asia and the concept of an Asian Economic Community in which India might play a leading role (Batra, 2004). While these ideas are not practical in the foreseeable future, since they do not connect with exactly what is going on in East Asia and the conditions that would be necessary to realise an Asian Economic Community, the foundations are being laid for India to become a significant player in the Asia Pacific economy.

What Sort of Asian Economic Community?

What sort of Asian Economic Community is practical and how might India's role in it evolve?

The scale of Indian development, developments in China and East Asia and the growing interaction between the two indicate that there are many issues that will bring closer both these subregions in Asia. But neither East Asia nor the two great subregions are remotely ready for institutional integration, even in the form of a comprehensive free trade area. Such is the scale of their impact on world markets that their priority—as with Japan and East Asia in an earlier time—must be for global solutions in global forums. This priority needs to shape their approach to regional action. Moreover, as Soesastro (2006) concludes, "the East Asian Summit does not represent a significant move beyond ASEAN+3. If countries such as India and Australia, which are new to the East Asian process, can take a high profile, this could well produce a new, exciting process. India's Prime Minister Manmohan Singh, talked about the East Asian Summit as a first step towards an East Asian Community (EAC), which will evolve into an Asian Economic Community (AEC). But it is unlikely that India and Australia will be allowed to 'hi-jack' the process."

So APEC and, now to a lesser extent, ASEAN+3 are still the key instruments of East Asian and Pacific Economic Cooperation and are likely to remain so for some time.

APEC's rationale today is not in dealing with the accommodation of Japan's rise but in dealing with the rise of China's economic and political reach and the locus of economic power in East Asia centred on China and Japan. The Shanghai Summit was symbolic of this development (APEC, 2001; Zhang, 2000; Drysdale, 2005a). One option is that India may join the club. As of now, APEC provides a broad and helpful framework for economic and political dialogues between China, the United States, Japan, ASEAN and all their Asia Pacific partners, including Russia. The dynamic of China's rise on the region's economic and political transformation was bound to make it so (Drysdale, 1988; Drysdale and Terada, 2006). India's participation in the East Asian Summit makes it a more likely candidate for APEC.

For all the activity and bureaucratic energy that have been directed towards bilateral trade diplomacy in Asia and across the Pacific, the results thus far have been trivial, and may remain so given the structure of Asia's intra-regional and extra-regional trade and economic interests. The location of relatively labour-intensive component production and assembly within complex, integrated international production and service chains has been a growing feature of the international division of labour, especially in East Asia. This process of broader and deeper integration is at the heart of East Asia's and China's successful trade and economic transformation. If they became deeply entrenched, discriminatory trade arrangements with their complicated rules of origin would contradict and undermine this style of deep and successful economic integration in East Asia (Drysdale, 2005b). What is true for East Asia is also increasingly true for India.

The evolution of Asian economic cooperation arrangements does not depend on the success of bilateral preferential trade strategies. There is a large agenda beyond the pursuit of FTAs, or even a comprehensive East Asian FTA, around which East Asian economic dialogues have, and can, be structured. Given the internal tensions within East Asia (such as those between China and Japan) the successful promotion of East Asian regionalism is more likely if it is encompassed within a broader framework like APEC that encourages continuing US engagement in the region and in which the engagement of India is viewed not merely as a political tactic but rather as a partner for substantial economic reasons.

There are two aspects of the agenda for cooperation in Asia and the Pacific in the future that require some final comment (Elek, 2005a and 2005b). The first relates to how the region can contribute to unravelling the mess that has developed in the form of discriminatory trade policy and invigorate the momentum of regional economic reform. This is an issue of immense importance to India. The second relates to how the region deals with the challenges of East Asian arrangements and refocuses its economic agenda to promote Asia Pacific prosperity.

APEC was never designed to be a negotiating forum on trade liberalisation or any other issues; neither was ASEAN+3 or the East Asian Summit. While there are still those in North America (Bergsten, 2005) and elsewhere who continue to dream of an Asia Pacific Free Trade Area and the institutionalisation of APEC within an FTA framework, this strategy defies reality. The dynamic of economic and political development in Asia and the Pacific promises only the most destructive outcome for any attempt at negotiating a transregional arrangement of this kind (Drysdale, 2005a). APEC's trade liberalisation focus remains clearly on invigorating and strengthening the WTO. The mess of counterproductive bilateral FTAs emerging in the region demands that priority be accorded to developing rules and strategies within the WTO and within APEC that serve to open FTAs in a way that promotes multilateral trade liberalisation and limits their discriminatory effects (Garnaut, 2004). Most of the benefits of trade liberalisation are realised by the economy that reduces border barriers to trade. Hence, support for unilateral economic reform and trade liberalisation in the structure of APEC, though recently out of favour, remains an important priority for Asian economies, especially India and China.

There is, however, a more important economic agenda on which the region now needs to focus. As Dee (2005) has demonstrated persuasively, the biggest gains from economic reform in East Asia, and, indeed, throughout the Asia Pacific region, come from behind-the-border regulatory reform. As Dee (2005) argues, the big gains are to be had from reforming the non-discriminatory restrictions on competition that affect both foreigners and domestic new entrants equally. This is best done through domestic initiative, where the debate can be held about how any losses to incumbents can be managed politically. The economies within APEC and the East Asian arrangements could provide important moral support, and 'benchmark' each other in these domestic initiatives. The numbers Dee (2005) generates are, indeed, striking—gains of more than five times those that might be available through a comprehensive East Asian FTA (Table 2.2). Behind-the-border reform, of course, is often closely linked to, and reinforces, trade reform. Progress with behind-the-border regulatory reform cannot easily be negotiated within any current international or regional forum. It is a challenge for independent action by national governments. But there are certainly institutional settings at a national level in which progress is more likely and there is a key role for APEC support and capacity building that encourages common purpose in the pursuit of regulatory reform. Efforts on this and other fronts might also provide opportunity for institutional innovation within the region putting in place decentralised regional cooperation processes that carry their main agendas under the umbrella of leaders' and ministers' meetings. The most effective way to tackle remaining border barriers is through the WTO. APEC or East Asian arrangements, on the other hand, can be used to facilitate both trade and investment, especially if some Asia Pacific economies set practical examples which others are encouraged to follow.

Table 2.2

Reform Scenarios and their Effects on East Asian Welfare

(Deviation from Control in Real Income, Measured in US$ billion per year)

Sector	*East Asian Economic Integration*	*Possible Round Outcome*	*Doha Comprehensive Unilateral Regulatory Reform*
Regulatory (services investment)	Reform national Treatment in and East Asia	National treatment in the world	Reform of all non-discriminatory regulation in East Asia
	1.7	7.4	107.3
Manufacturing tariffs	Elimination of Tariffs against East Asian Partners	25 per cent reduction in tariffs globally	
	16.6	12.4	
Agricultural protection	No action	25 per cent reduction in agricultural protection globally	
	0.0	12.8	
Total	**18.3**	**32.6**	**107.3**

Source: Dee (2005: 17), FTAP model projections.

It might be thought that a role model exists in the European Single Market Agenda that generated very substantial new benefits after its introduction in 1992 (Drysdale, 2005a; Elek, 2005b), complementing the free trade agreement that Europe has had in place from the late 1960s. While analogous to the EU's Single Market Agenda, it will make more sense for a single market agenda in Asia and the Pacific to be implemented in a way that suits the much more diverse group of economies that comprise this region, rather than focus on achieving a 'single regional market' at some target date. The implementation of this agenda can be sequenced ahead of or alongside and not necessarily after, border trade liberalisation (as it was in the case of Europe). Major elements of this agenda are already underway in the context of APEC's work on trade facilitation; this work can be intensified and new elements added as proposed at the Busan Summit. This approach is well suited to APEC's capabilities. It is consistent with WTO principles and will take APEC a long way down the path to the Bogor goals. It constitutes a package of initiatives for market integration in the broadest sense, and these initiatives can be pursued in tandem with ongoing multilateral, regional and bilateral trade liberalisation efforts. In Asia and the Pacific there would sensibly be no attempt to impose a programme of reforms upon those participating but a priority would be to buttress the policy institutions and capacities that encourage and benchmark regulatory and trade reforms. These strategies can help to invigorate and refocus the regional cooperation agenda in the years immediately ahead.

Conclusion

Over the last half century, the East Asian and Pacific economy has been the centre of one of the most remarkable transformations in world economy in modern times. Building policy consensus on how to manage the international economic dimensions of this position, and articulating it through APEC, has played a not unimportant role in keeping this achievement on track. The success of East Asia's trade and economic transformation is in part a significant achievement of international economic diplomacy, both within the global system and through innovation in regional economic cooperation. The huge economic and political changes that are being swept along by the third great wave of East Asian industrialisation, and the emergence of South Asia as a major centre of world economic growth, present new opportunities for extending this success. While India continues to build its links with East Asian partners through the East Asian Summit and bilateral economic diplomacy, the promotion of an Asian Economic Community which supports reform-driven outward-looking growth and helps to manage the deeper integration in regional and world markets that accompany it may usefully be related to the broader economic cooperation agenda within APEC. APEC continues to play a positive role in reducing these risks and improving regional outcomes in both their economic and political dimensions. The time will soon be ripe for India to join the APEC process.

References

APEC (2001). *Economic Leaders' Declaration*. Shanghai.

———. (1995). *Economic Leaders' Declaration for Action*. Osaka.

———. (1994). *Economic Leaders' Declaration of Common Resolve*. Bogor.

———. (1993). *Leaders Economic Vision Statement*. Seattle.

Batra, Amita (2004). "Response to East Asian Regionalism and Its Impact—The Indian View". *(mimeo)*. New Delhi: ICRIER. November.

Bergsten, C. Fred (1994). "APEC and the World Economy: A Force for Worldwide Liberalisation", *Foreign Affairs*, Vol. 73(3): 20-26. May/June.

———. (2005). "Rescuing the Doha Round", *Foreign Affairs*, December, p.4.

———. (1997). "Open Regionalism", *World Economy*, Vol. 20(5): 545-65.

Bonner, Jenelle (1996). "APEC's Contribution to Regional Security", in H. Soesastro and A. Bergin (eds.), *The Role of Security and Economic Cooperation Structures in the Asia Pacific Region: Indonesian and Australian Views*. Jakarta: Centre for Strategic and International Studies. pp.45-56.

Chidambaram, P. (2006). *India's Perspectives on Regional Cooperation in Asia*. Manila: ADB. 16 January.

Dee, Philippa (2005). "East Asian Economic Integration and Its Impact on Future Growth", *Pacific Economic Papers*, ANU, No. 350. Canberra: Australia-Japan Research Centre, p.18.

Drysdale, Peter (2005a). "East Asian FTAs and APEC's Bogor Goals", *East Asian Regionalism and its Impact*. Beijing: Institute of Asia and the Pacific, Chinese Academy of Social Sciences.

———. (2005b), "Regional Cooperation in East Asia and FTA Strategies", *Pacific Economic Papers*, No. 344. Canberra. pp.1-20.

———. (1988). *International Economic Pluralism: Economic Policy in East Asia and the Pacific*. Sydney: Allen & Unwin and Columbia University Press.

Drysdale, Peter and Andrew Elek (1997). "APEC: Community-Building in East Asia and the Pacific", in D.C. Hellmann and K.B. Pyle (eds.), *From APEC to Xanadu: Creating a Viable Community in the Post-war Pacific*. M.E. Armonk: Sharpe. pp.37-69.

Drysdale, Peter and Ross Garnaut (1993). "The Pacific: An Application of a General Theory of Economic Integration", in C. Fred Bergsten and Marcus Noland (eds.), *Pacific Dynamism and the International Economic System*. Washington, D.C.: Institute of International Economics. pp.183-223.

Drysdale, Peter, Yiping Huang and Kali P. Kalirajan (2000). "China's Trade Efficiency: Measurement and Determinants", in Peter Drysdale, Yunling Zhang and Ligang Song (eds.), *APEC and Liberalisation of the Chinese Economy*. Canberra: Asia Pacific Press.

Drysdale, Peter and Kenichi Ishigaki (2002). "New Issues in East Asian Integration", in Peter Drysdale and Kenichi Ishigaki (eds.), *East Asian Trade and Financial Integration: New Issues*. Canberra: Asia Pacific Press. pp.3-12.

Drysdale, Peter and Hugh Patrick (1979). "An Asian-Pacific Regional Economic Organisation: An Exploratory Concept Paper". Washington DC: US Government Printing Office, US Congressional Research Service. July.

Drysdale, Peter and Takashi Terada (2006). *APEC: Critical Perspectives on the World Economy*, Volumes 1-5. London: Routledge. (forthcoming).

Drysdale, Peter and Xinpeng Xu (2004). "Taiwan's Role in the Economic Architecture of East Asia and the Pacific", *Pacific Economic Papers*, No. 343. Canberra: Australia–Japan Research Centre. p.34.

Drysdale, Peter, Yunling Zhang and Ligang Song (2000). *APEC and Liberalisation of the Chinese Economy*. Canberra: Asia Pacific Press.

Elek, Andrew (2005a). *APEC After Busan: New Direction*. Seoul: The Korea Institute of International Economic Policy, p.114.

———. (2005b). "The Mid-term Review of the Bogor Goals: Strategic Issues and Options", in *The Future of APEC and Regionalism in the Asia Pacific: Perspectives from the Second Track*. Singapore and Jakarta: Pacific Economic Cooperation Council and the Centre for Strategic and International Studies. April.

Findlay, Christopher (2002). "Walking and Chewing Gum at the Same Time: Australia's Free Trade Area Strategy". *The Australian Journal of Agricultural and Resource Economics*, Vol. 46(4): 605-17. December.

Garnaut, Ross (2004). "A New Open Regionalism in Asia and the Pacific", paper presented to the *International Conference on the World Economy*. 25 November. Colima, Mexico.

———. (2000). "APEC Ideas and Reality: History and Prospects", in I. Yamazawa (ed.), *APEC: Its Challenges and Tasks in the 21st Century*. New York, Routledge. pp.1-18.

———. (1996). "Open Regionalism: Its Analytic Basis and Relevance to the International System", in Ross Garnaut (ed.), *Open Regionalism and Trade Liberalisation: An Asia-Pacific Contribution to the World Trade System*. Sydney: Allen & Unwin. pp.16-41.

Gordon, Bernard (2003). "A High-Risk Trade Policy", *Foreign Affairs*, Vol. 82(4): 105-18. July/August.

Harris, Stuart (2000). "Asian Multilateral Institutions and their Response to the Asian Economic Crisis: The Regional and Global Implications", *The Pacific Review*, Vol. 13(3): 495-516.

MacIntyre, Andrew and Hadi Soesastro (2005). "Politico-Strategic Dimensions of Economic Cooperation in the Asia Pacific", in Christopher Findlay and Hadi Soesastro (eds.), *Reshaping the Asia Pacific Economic Order*. London: Routledge.

Munakata, Naoko (2001). "Evolution of Japan's Policy Toward Economic Integration", *CNAPS Working Paper*. The Brookings Institution. December (also cited as RIETI Discussion Paper Series 02-E-006).

Ohira, Masayoshi (1980). "Creative Partnership for the Pacific Age", Luncheon Speech. (*mimeo*). Melbourne. 17 January.

Pacific Community Seminar (1981). "Origins of the Pacific Community", in J.G. Crawford and G. Seow (ed.), *Pacific Economic Cooperation: Suggestions for Action*. Heinemann Asia, for the *Pacific Community Seminar*. Selangor: Petaling Jaya. pp.101-05.

Singh, Manmohan (2005). *Keynote Address by the Indian Prime Minister to Special Leaders' Dialogues of the ASEAN Business Advisory Council*. Kuala Lumpur. December.

Sen, Rahul (2005). "ASEAN-India", Workshop on *Investment and Services Strategies for ASEAN FTAs'*. Singapore: Institute of South East Asian Studies. 8 November.

Soesastro, Hadi (2006). "East Asia: Many Clubs, Little Progress", *Far Eastern Economic Review*, Vol. 169(1): 50-53, January/February.

———. (2001). "Towards an East Asian Regional Trading Arrangement", in S.C. Tay, H. Soesastro and J.P. Estanislao (eds.), *Reinventing ASEAN*. Singapore: Institute of South East Asian Studies. pp.226-42.

———. (1994). "Pacific Economic Cooperation: The History of an Idea", in Ross Garnaut and Peter Drysdale (eds.), *Asia Pacific Regionalism: Readings in International Economic Relations*. Sydney: Harper Educational. pp.77-88.

Terada, Takashi (1999). "The Genesis of APEC: Australia–Japan Political Initiatives", *Pacific Economic Papers*, No. 298. December. pp.7-51.

Wesley, Michael (2001). "APEC's Mid-life Crisis? The Rise and Fall of Early Voluntary Sectoral Liberalisation", *Pacific Affairs*, Vol. 74(2): 185-204. Summer.

Yamazawa, Ippei (1992). "On Pacific Economic Integration", *The Economic Journal*, Vol. 102(415): 1519-29, November.

Zhang, Yunling (2000). "Liberalisation of the Chinese Economy: APEC, WTO and Tariff Reductions", in Peter Drysdale, Yunling Zhang and Ligang Song (eds.), *APEC and Liberalisation of the Chinese Economy*. Canberra: Asia Pacific Press. pp.3-14.

3

Preferential Trading Agreements in Asia

Towards an Asian Economic Community

AMITA BATRA

Introduction

In Asia, the drive towards regionalism gained momentum in the 1990s when many countries in the region announced their intention to form bilateral and regional trade agreements. In 1998, there was initial discussion on a Japan–Korea trade agreement. This was followed, in quick succession, by the launching of trade initiatives by Korea, Singapore, Japan, China and ASEAN. There has been a proliferation in bilateral and plurilateral as also intra-regional and extra-regional agreements by ASEAN, its member nations, East Asian economies and India. The region is also actively pursuing initiatives to extend the existing regional agreements to include additional countries. Among these are agreements between the ASEAN regional grouping and Japan (AJCEP), China (ACCEC), Republic of Korea[1] (AKCCP) and India (AICEC). The framework agreement has been signed for all these initiatives. A further initiative at forming a preferential trade agreement (PTA) comprising ASEAN+3 is under discussion and is seen by many as the building block of a future East Asian Community (EAC). The EAC can then become the harbinger of the Asian Economic Community (AEC) as envisioned by India. A step in the direction of regional partnership that is inclusive of ASEAN+3+3 [ASEAN+(Japan, China and Korea)+(India, Australia and New Zealand)] has already been taken through the recently held East Asia Summit (EAS). As revealed during the deliberations, the aim of the EAS is to ultimately establish an integrated economic community in Asia on the lines of the European Union (EU).

1. Hereafter Korea.

Preferential trading arrangements (PTAs) among economies in any region have, however, raised several concerns. A primary concern is if the PTA implies an efficiency cost and if it will, as a consequence, undermine trade liberalisation through the multilateral process. Given that a PTA accords preferential treatment to members *vis-a-vis* non-members there is always a possibility of trade being diverted away from non-members to members. On occasion when non-members are more efficient producers this process of trade diversion will imply a cost in terms of denying both the producers and the consumers access to lower cost and more efficiently produced goods. A preferential trading arrangement, therefore, needs to be evaluated to determine if there are efficiency costs by way of distortion in the patterns of trade away from those expected on the basis of comparative advantage.

Having regard to this background of regional economic integration in Asia and the concerns raised on efficiency costs there is a need to undertake an analysis of the proposed new regional arrangement in Asia. It is in this context that we set out the research agenda for this paper. Understanding the efficiency implications of the preferential trading arrangement will help policymakers in the participating countries to better prepare for and cope with economic integration in the region and evaluate the worth of the formation of future PTAs *vis-a-vis* multilateral liberalisation.

For the purpose of our analysis we define Asia as inclusive of ASEAN, the plus three economies of China, Japan, Korea, and India, that is, the ASEAN+4.[2] Given that ASEAN is an existing regional bloc in Asia, alternative approaches to the alignment of the plus four economies with ASEAN for the formation of the ASEAN+4 trade bloc are examined in terms of their efficiency costs. As a first step to our analysis, however, we establish the economic credentials of ASEAN+4 as a potential candidate for regional economic integration in Asia.

---

2. The ASEAN-Australia and New Zealand FTA i.e. AFTA-CER CEP has trade facilitation rather than trade liberalisation as its agenda. Our analysis is, therefore, restricted to 14 of the 16 countries that were represented in the East Asia Summit in December 2005.

The analysis is undertaken for the period 1999-2003 as the drive towards regionalism in Asia gained momentum only after the 1997-1998 East Asian crisis. For the purpose of comparison, where required, the analysis has also been undertaken for the period 1995-1999. UNCOMTRADE based trade data classified according to the Harmonised System (HS) at the 2- and 6-digit levels have been used for analysis.

Selected Review of Literature

Several studies have examined the idea of regional economic integration in Asia. Most of these studies have focused on separate regions of ASEAN, North East Asia (the plus three economies of China, Japan and Korea) and the ASEAN+3. Mingqui (2003) has analysed the ASEAN+3 region for economic integration. In his study Mingqui provides evidence of increased interdependence among the 13 economies in the area of trade, capital flows and human resource mobility in support of economic integration in the region. Asian Development Bank (ADB, 2005) presents data indicative of the extent of trade and investment integration in Asia by subregions like East Asia and South Asia. In the study East Asia is defined as the ASEAN 10 and the PRC, Japan, Korea, Hong Kong, China and Taipei, China. The extent of regional integration has been indicated on the basis of the intra-regional trade and investment shares and intensity measures. A large number of studies, however, deal with the impact of trade bloc formation in terms of welfare and economic gains by undertaking *ex post* analysis using the gravity model, e.g. Lee, Park and Shin (2004) and/or an *ex ante* analysis using CGE techniques.[3] The most comprehensive study, by Scollay and Gilbert (2001), highlights the small benefits associated with bilateral arrangements and points out the damage that some of them could inflict upon member and non-member nations.

---

3. For example, Scollay and Gilbert (2001) and Yamazawa (2001) have estimated the potential effect of FTAs in North East Asia on welfare, trade and productivity.

A systematic comparison or assessment of the many arrangements that have been proposed for economic integration in Asia has, however, not been undertaken so far. Studies on the efficiency of alternative regional arrangements or on the strategy of optimal sequencing of regional economic integration in Asia are missing. Furthermore, India does not find a mention in the limited number of impact studies undertaken for Asian FTAs. Even where options for economic integration of ASEAN-East Asia that are inclusive of India are considered the focus remains on simplistic statements on India's complementarities with East Asia in the services sector and the emerging trends of India's competitive advantage as an outsourcing hub in the region.[4] The focus of this study is at variance with issues discussed in the available literature as it aims at identifying the most efficient approach to the formation of a regional trade arrangement in Asia that is inclusive of India.

ASEAN+4 as a Potential Trade Bloc

The ASEAN+4 region comprising two of the most dynamic economies in the world, that is, India and China, has been referred to as the "Arc of Advantage" by the Indian Prime Minister. As may be noticed, from the available facts presented in Table 3.1, the gross national income of the countries comprising this regional bloc is over US$ 7.6 trillion in 2003 and is comparable to the US$ 9.4 trillion gross national income of the EU. In terms of purchasing power parity (PPP), the national income of ASEAN+4 is US$ 16 trillion and is more than the national income of the North American Free Trade Agreement (NAFTA) which is US$ 13 trillion or of the EU which is US$ 11 trillion. The combined total reserves of this region are about US$ 2 trillion, and are much larger than that of the EU. Given that the proposed 14-country singular economic entity of ASEAN+4 has a 19 per cent share in total world trade, which is almost as much as that of NAFTA and contributes 21 per cent of the global output and is, in addition, home to about half of the world's population, it has the potential to impact the global as well as the regional economies.

---

4. The strengthening of India's linkages with ASEAN-5, in particular finds a mention in Rajan and Sen in ADB (2005). The context, however, remains as the 'increasing complementarities in the services sector'.

Table 3.1

ASEAN+4 Region: Summary Indicators

	ASEAN+4	*NAFTA*	*EU*
Gross National Income (trillion US$)	7.6	12.5	9.4
National Income (trillion US$) PPP	16.0	13.0	11.0
Population (billion)	3.03	0.42	0.45
Total Reserves (trillion US$)	1.6	0.25	0.52
Share of World Trade (Per cent)	19.22	20.27	38.8

Source: World Bank (2005). *WDI.*

Trends in Intra-regional Trade

The case for ASEAN+4 as a potential trade bloc in Asia is proposed on the basis of the encouraging trends evident in intra-bloc trade. Intra-regional trade as a per cent of total trade at an aggregate level for the ASEAN+4 economies along with some selected blocs is shown in Table 3.2.[5] Trade among the member nations of ASEAN+4 as against their trade with the rest of the world registered an increase in the period 1995-2003 even though there was a fall in 1999, possibly on account of the East Asian crisis. In 2003 intra-bloc trade for ASEAN+4 was 44 per cent. This value of intra-regional trade share is higher than the corresponding share for many of the existing trade blocs in the year of their formation. For example, intra-bloc trade for NAFTA was 42.1 per cent in 1994 and for Mercusor it was 12.9 per cent in 1991.[6]

Table 3.2

Intra-bloc Trade

(Per cent)

Regions	*1995*	*1999*	*2003*
ASEAN	25.5	24.6	25.3
ASEAN+4	42.0	39.5	44.0
NAFTA	45.0	50.1	49.9

Note: All tables, unless otherwise specified, are based on author's calculations.

5. Data has been presented at four-year intervals to reduce the influence of any annual irregular variations such as those on account of fluctuations in commodity prices.
6. Schiff and Winters (2003).

It is also evident from Table 3.2 that the potential of ASEAN+4 as a candidate for regional economic integration is higher than that of the existing regional bloc in Asia, that is, ASEAN. Intra-ASEAN trade is less than that of ASEAN+4. This fact is further corroborated when the trends for intra-bloc exports and imports, shown in Tables 3.3 and 3.4, are analysed. There exists a positive difference between the levels of intra-bloc exports and imports for the proposed ASEAN+4 grouping as against the existing ASEAN. In 2003, intra-ASEAN trade–both exports and imports stood at 22 per cent and this is much lower than the 35 per cent and 43 per cent of intra-ASEAN+4 exports and imports, respectively.

Table 3.3

Intra-bloc Exports

(Per Cent)

Year	*1995*	*1999*	*2003*
ASEAN	25.5	22.5	22.4
ASEAN+4	35.2	31.1	35.0

Table 3.4

Intra-bloc Imports

(Per Cent)

Year	*1995*	*1999*	*2003*
ASEAN	17.5	21.8	22.0
ASEAN+4	38.9	39.8	43.0

Trends in intra-regional trade are, therefore, suggestive of the strength of the ASEAN+4 as a potential candidate for a regional bloc in Asia.[7] This conclusion is further substantiated when the degree of 'trade bias' among member nations of the proposed bloc is evaluated using the index of trade intensity (TI).

7. A series of earlier papers like Wonnacott and Lutz (1989), Summers (1991), Krugman (1993) and Frankel, Stein and Wei (1995) argue that RTAs with larger pre–trade volumes and geographically proximate countries are likely to be welfare improving. Member nations of RTAs are referred to as 'natural trading partners' based on the criterion of the volume of trade. The volume of trade, may not, even though it is the most popular criterion, necessarily provide an objective measure of the extent to which the trading partners are 'natural' given that the volume of trade is itself affected by trade policy.

Intra-regional Trade Intensity

Increases in intra-regional trade signify an increase in interdependence but do not give a strong indication of the 'bias' towards regionalisation, as they may reflect changes in other variables, especially income growth (Petri, 1992). The growth in internal trade shares may, therefore, reflect income-induced changes in imports, rather than a rise in 'natural' tendency to trade. To control this effect, the TI index normalises the bilateral or intra-regional trade shares according to the importance of the country or region in total world trade. The index of trade intensity with a value greater than one is indicative of higher bilateral trade than can be expected on the basis of the countries' share in world trade. The change in the value of the index over time reveals if any two countries/groupings are experiencing an increased or decreased tendency to trade with one another. An increasing value of the index is indicative of enhanced prospects for further integration while a decreasing value would suggest diminished prospects. The TI index therefore, provides additional insights into the prospects for regional economic integration.

Table 3.5

Intra-regional Trade Intensity Index

Regions	*1995*	*1999*	*2003*
ASEAN	3.9	4.5	4.4
ASEAN+4	2.1	2.2	2.2
NAFTA	2.4	2.3	2.7

Table 3.5 summarises the change in the TI index[8] at three time points[9] in our reference period. For a comparative picture the TI indices at the same time points are also shown for NAFTA. The TI

8. Intra-ASEAN Trade Intensity equals: (Intra-ASEAN Exports/Total World Exports)/ {(Total ASEAN Exports/Total World Exports)*(World Exports to ASEAN/Total World Exports)}: Kawai (2004)

9. A limitation that is often cited of the TI index is that it fails to account for the distance between individual countries. Ng and Yeats (2003) have calculated the distance adjusted TI at a time point. The calculation of the TI over three different time points in our analysis should take care of this as bilateral distance remains constant over the period of time.

index for ASEAN+4 clearly documents the increase in the concentration of trade within the region. The TI index as shown in Table 3.5 exceeds unity for all the three time points in our reference period. This is indicative of 'intense' trade relations within the ASEAN+4 regional grouping.[10] The TI index for ASEAN+4 is comparable to that for NAFTA, particularly at the time of the latter's coming into effect.[11] Trends in the index of trade intensity further confirm the claim of ASEAN+4 as a potential candidate for a regional trade bloc in Asia.

Potential for Trade Creation

The potential impact of the ASEAN+4 bloc is further reinforced when analysed for its trade creation effects using an augmented gravity model. Extending the Batra (2006) gravity model to include additional dummy variables for ASEAN+4 as a trade bloc, it is found that the ASEAN+4 trade bloc can potentially create three times the actual trade between India and ASEAN, China, Japan and Korea. Analysis of the net trade creation effect of the proposed regional arrangement for individual member countries reveals that the maximum trade potential for India is with China and can be four times the current levels.

While available trends on intra-ASEAN+4 trade establish the strength of the group by itself and relative to the existing bloc in Asia, that is, ASEAN, for regional economic integration, there is a need to ascertain the relative positioning of India *vis-à-vis* the other three economies. The need to contextualise India in the proposed bloc becomes evident when we look at the share of each of the plus four economies in intra-ASEAN+4 trade (Table 3.6). It is observed that currently India makes the lowest contribution to intra-regional trade (exports and imports) for the proposed trade bloc. In 2003, in comparison with Japan that has the maximum share of 28 and 25 per cent in total regional exports and imports, respectively, India's share

10. Relative to ASEAN the TI index for ASEAN+4 that is inclusive of China, Japan, Korea and India is smaller in magnitude as the TI indices control for a region's relative size in world trade.

11. This corroborates earlier evidence in favour of the ASEAN+4. Intra-regional trade shares for ASEAN+4 in contrast with that of ASEAN are comparable to that for NAFTA at the time of the latter's formation.

at about 2.0 and 3.0 per cent in exports and imports, respectively, is the lowest.

Table 3.6

Share of the +4 Economies in Intra-ASEAN+4 Exports and Imports

(Per Cent)

Countries	*Share in Intra-ASEAN+4 Exports*		*Share in Intra-ASEAN+4 Imports*	
	1999	*2003*	*1999*	*2003*
China	15.7	20.3	18.7	27.8
India	1.4	2	2.9	2.8
Japan	30.1	27.8	30.1	25.4
Korea	14.2	13.5	12.9	12.8

However, India's alignment with ASEAN+4 is justifiable on account of the rate at which the latter's trade with India is growing relative to that with the plus three economies, increased share *vis-à-vis* other major trading blocs and partner countries in India's total trade and the growing importance of India as a market for exports of ASEAN+4 economies. In the following section we present evidence in support of India's increasing trade linkages with the proposed bloc.

The Case for India in ASEAN+4

Rate of Growth of Total Trade with ASEAN+4

The rate of growth of total trade of the plus four economies with ASEAN+4 is presented in Table 3.7. It is observed that the rate of

Table 3.7

Rate of Growth of Total Trade with ASEAN+4

(Per Cent)

Year	*India*	*China*	*Japan*	*Korea*
1999-2000	-3.2	33.0	28.3	31.2
2000-2001	11.4	5.4	-9.5	-11.8
2001-2002	24.8	21.9	5.3	13.2
2002-2003	37.3	37.4	20.6	23.8
Average Annual Rate of Growth	9.5	12.7	3.0	5.3

growth of India's total trade with ASEAN+4 over 1999–2003 is close to that of China and greater than that of Japan and Korea. Among the plus four economies India registered the highest annual rate of growth of total trade with ASEAN+4 over the period 2001-2003.

Trade with ASEAN+4 vis-à-vis other Regional Blocs

India's trade with regional blocs presents an interesting picture (Table 3.8). In 1995, the EU (15/25) was the most significant trading bloc for India in terms of its share in total trade. Trade with the EU constituted 28 per cent of India's total trade. This was followed by NAFTA at around 15 per cent and ASEAN at 8 per cent. In 2003, the share of EU in India's total trade fell to 21 per cent and the share of the proposed ASEAN+4 bloc increased to about 20 per cent.[12] With its share in India's total trade having increased to equal that of the EU, ASEAN+4 has emerged as the other dominant partner bloc for India.

Table 3.8

Shares of Select Trade Blocs in India's Total Trade

(Per Cent)

Year	*EU15*	*EU25*	*NAFTA*	*Mercosur*	*ASEAN*	*ASEAN+4*	*SAARC*
1995	27.4	28.0	14.9	0.8	7.8	**18.1**	2.9
1999	23.5	24.0	15.2	1.1	8.5	**17.5**	2.1
2003	20.2	20.7	12.9	0.9	9.3	**19.9**	3.4

Trade with ASEAN+4 vis-à-vis Rest of the World

India's trade orientation towards the proposed trade bloc is also apparent when we look at the increasing divergence between the shares of ASEAN+4 and the rest of the world in India's total trade. As is evident from Figure 3.1, there is a clear increase in the share of ASEAN+4 in India's total trade at the expense of the rest of the world. Over the period 2000–03 the share of ASEAN+4 in India's total trade

12. It may be noted that the share of ASEAN in India's total trade has remained at about the same level over 1995-2003.

has increased from 15 to almost 20 per cent and that of rest of the world registered a fall from 85 to 80 per cent.

Figure 3.1

Share of ASEAN+4 Versus Rest of the World (ROW) in India's Total Trade

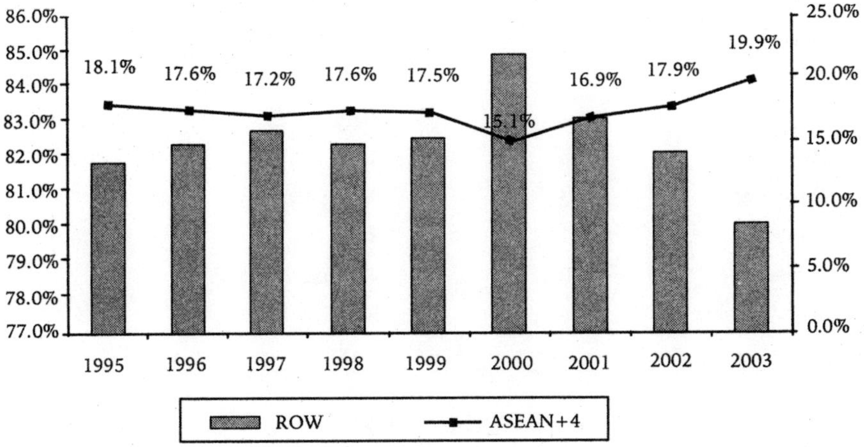

As concerns individual member nations, in 2003, three of the ASEAN+4 countries–China, Japan and Singapore—feature among the top ten trading partners for India. Singapore and China first emerged among the top ten trading partners for India in 2000 and have remained so since then. China has over the same period emerged as the third largest trading partner for India (Table 3.9).

India as a Market for the ASEAN+4

Simultaneous with the increase in the share of ASEAN+4 in India's total trade it is observed that there is an increase in India's relevance for the ASEAN+4 nations. Evidence shows that India is increasingly being looked at as a market for exports (Table 3.10). Over the years 1995-2003 India registered the highest rate of growth in the region for Chinese and Indonesian exports. India is second only to China as the most attractive market in the region for Korean, Malaysian and Thai exports.

Table 3.9

India's Top Ten Trading Partners

Top Ten 2003	*Share 2003 (Per cent)*	*Top Ten 1995*	*Share 1995 (Per cent)*
USA	11.7	USA	13.7
UAE	5.0	Germany	7.5
China	4.9	*Japan*	6.8
UK	4.4	UK	5.7
Belgium	4.1	Belgium-Lux.	4.1
Germany	3.8	UAE	3.9
Hong Kong	3.3	Hong Kong	3.2
Japan	3.1	Italy	2.8
Singapore	3.0	Russian Fed.	2.7
Switz. Leicht.	2.6	Saudi Arabia	2.7

Note: Countries in italics are members of ASEAN+4.

Table 3.10

India as a Market for ASEAN+4: A Comparison with the +3 Economies

Markets	*Bru. Dar.*	*China*	*India*	*Indon.*	*Japan*	*Korea*	*Malay.*	*Phili.*	*Singap.*	*Thai.*
China	–	–	86.7	13.1	17.9	31.6	27.6	–	29.7	27.5
India	–	37.4	–	39.7	-0.6	17.0	22.8	–	7.2	13.5
Japan	–	12.1	-2.6	1.2	–	6.1	2.2	–	0.6	2.3
Korea Rep.	–	22.3	7.7	5.4	1.3		5.3		9.6	11.0

Note: Figures in the table represent average annual rate of growth of exports to the specific markets over 1999-2003.

The fact that India is emerging as an important market for intra-regional exports is corroborated when we look at India's trade with ASEAN+4. It may be seen from Table 3.11 that the average annual rate of growth of imports of India from ASEAN+4 exceeds the rate of growth of India's exports to ASEAN+4. In addition, when compared with other plus four economies, the rate of growth of India's imports from ASEAN+4 is second to China and significantly higher than that of Japan and Korea.

Table 3.11

Rate of Growth of Exports and Imports of the +4 Economies: 1995-2003

	India	*China*	*Japan*	*Korea*
Imports from ASEAN+4	10.8	14.6	4.4	4.8
Exports to ASEAN+4	7.7	10.5	1.7	5.8

Having thus noted the justification for India's inclusion in the proposed bloc, we analyse if India can be positioned in a manner similar to the +3 economies or if there are any features characterising India that make it distinct from the other three economies and which may have implications for trade integration in Asia. For this purpose we undertake a comparative analysis of the trade bias towards the proposed bloc as exhibited by India and the plus three economies.

India vis-à-vis the +3 Economies

It is observed that the share of trade with ASEAN+4 in total trade, exports and imports is far greater for the plus three economies than for India. In 2003, the share of ASEAN+4 in Korea's total trade is 41 per cent, double the region's share of 20 per cent in India's total trade. Corresponding shares for China and Japan are 33 and 36 per cent, respectively. Similar trends are observed for exports and imports (Table 3.12).

Table 3.12

Share of ASEAN+4 in Total Trade of the +4 Economies: 2003

	India	*China*	*Japan*	*Korea Rep.*
Total Trade	19.9	33.2	36.2	41.2
Exports	17.6	26.0	33.0	39.0
Imports	21.7	40.9	40.2	43.6

The TI index[13] further highlights the difference between India and the plus three economies *vis-à-vis* ASEAN+4. The TI index for each of the plus four economies with ASEAN+4 is presented in Table 3.13. The value of the TI index is close to 2 for all the +3 economies. This implies intense trade of these economies with ASEAN+4. In contrast the TI value of India with ASEAN+4 is yet to attain the value of unity. This suggests that unlike the plus three economies India does not at present reveal a marked trade bias towards the ASEAN+4.

Table 3.13

Trade Intensity Indices with ASEAN and ASEAN+4

	India	*Japan*	*Korea*	*China*
1995	1.2 (0.9)	2.4 (2.1)	1.9 (2.0)	0.9 (1.7)
1999	1.2 (0.8)	2.6 (2.1)	2.4 (2.3)	1.2 (2.1)
2003	1.7 (0.9)	2.4 (2.2)	1.8 (2.1)	1.1 (1.7)

Note: Numbers in parenthesis are TI indices for ASEAN+4.

So, India's trade with ASEAN+4 increasing at a rate greater than that of any of the plus three economies and its increasing importance as a market for ASEAN+4 provides the basis for accepting India as an integral part of ASEAN+4.[14] However, the share of the proposed bloc in the plus three economies' total trade is far greater than and more intense relative to its share in India's total trade. So a *de facto* market-led integration of the plus three economies with ASEAN (the

13. Following Kojima (1964) and Drysdale (1969), the index of trade intensity is defined for country i's exports to country j as the share of I's exports going to j(Xij/Xi) relative to the share of j's imports (Mj) in world imports net of I's imports (Mw-Mi). That is, Iij=(Xij/Xi)/ Mj/Mw-Mi.

14. India's trade intensity index with ASEAN+4 is less than one for aggregate trade. However, when a sector-wise TI index is calculated it is greater than one for sectors like agriculture and allied commodities, minerals and mineral fuels and more recently in the chemicals and plastics sector. Similar trends are evident from aggregate and sector-wise complementarity and bias indices, thus supporting our earlier inference on India's justified alignment with ASEAN+4.

ASEAN+3) is evident. In the ASEAN+4 set of countries India thus stands out as the 'distant' economy. For a trade bloc comprising the ASEAN, China, Japan, Korea and India it is, therefore, imperative that the path of integration for the 'distant' economy be identified. Considering that the index of trade intensity and bias is greater than unity for India-ASEAN trade over 1995-2003[15] we suggest that India should enter the ASEAN+4 by first aligning with ASEAN in an ASEAN+1 arrangement. This may happen through either of the following two options:[16]

a. ASEAN+1s: India's alignment on a plus one basis combined with all the plus three economies also entering through a plus one arrangement. A convergence of all the ASEAN+1 agreements will lead to the emergence of ASEAN+4; or

b. ASEAN+3+1: As stated above the ASEAN+3[17] already exists as a *de facto* market-led arrangement. India enters last through the ASEAN+1 route to constitute ASEAN+4.

We evaluate these two routes in terms of their efficiency costs using a two part methodology which is explained below.

Efficiency Costs

Alignment with ASEAN versus ASEAN+4

To estimate the efficiency costs associated with alignment of the plus four economies with ASEAN we examine if the additional trade that is generated on account of the anticipatory effects of the proposed/under negotiation/signed preferential arrangements is primarily in products in which these countries reveal comparative advantage in the global market. The analysis will allow us to infer if additional trade and increased export dynamism is in products where the plus four countries have low enough costs to be competitive in the

15. Refer Table 3.13.

16. For the plus three economies the index of trade intensity and bias show equal bias towards the existing and proposed bloc.

17. ASEAN+3 has been referred to as the most suitable candidate for East Asian regionalism in the literature (Baldwin, 2006; Drysdale, 2001). At this stage the ASEAN+3 group is not a regional trading agreement. The focus in ASEAN+3 is on financial cooperation.

world market. If this does not hold true then the comparison suggests that the additional trade within the respective markets/trading arrangements is inefficient, has attached costs and could have been replaced by more efficient outside suppliers.[18]

The investigation is undertaken using two indices—the index of revealed comparative advantage (RCA)[19] and the regional orientation (RO) index. The RO index conveys useful information about change in geographic patterns of trade as it takes the ratio of the share of a product in exports to the region to the share of the product in exports to third countries.[20] Both the index of RO and RCA are calculated at the 2-digit level of HS classification and for ASEAN+4 and ASEAN as target markets. As such, direct comparisons of the two indices provide an indication of the extent to which trade orientation towards ASEAN+4 and ASEAN distorts trade patterns based on comparative advantage in the global market[21] for each of the plus one economies. Efficiency costs are measured as the percentage of sectors in which the economy gets increasingly oriented towards the respective region over 1995-2003[22] even though it is not competitive in these sectors in the

---

18. The issue is essentially whether RTAs foster 'high cost' imports at the expense of 'low cost' ones. The traditional calculations of trade diversion based on import data infer this from the displacement of imports from non-partners by those from partners, implicitly comparing partner and non-partner costs by their relative competitiveness in the pre-RTA regional market. In this section we follow the supplementary view as developed in Yeats (1997) where inference about 'high' and 'low' costs is made by implicitly comparing the relative competitiveness of partner and non-partner goods in world markets.

19. The index of Revealed Comparative Advantage (RCA) is calculated as: RCAj = [xoj/X to]/[x*wj ÷ X*w].100 where x*wj and X*w represent world (ASEAN) exports of product j and total world exports respectively. xoj and X to represent country exports of j to world (ASEAN).

20. The regional orientation (RO) index is defined as:

    Rj = [xrj/X tr]/[xoj/Xto].100

    where xrj and xoj represent the value of exports of j to ASEAN and to ROW, respectively, and Xtr and Xto reflect the total value of the country's exports to ASEAN and outside the arrangement.

21. An attempt has also been made to do the same for the rest of the world market or the non-ASEAN world. The results are not significantly altered.

22. The change in RO index is calculated over a period of time as it conveys only limited information about trade patterns if computed for a single point in time. Inter-temporal comparisons over relatively short periods provide useful information on the way the geographic pattern of trade is changing.

global market. In other words, we identify the percentage number of sectors which satisfy the following criterion:

$(RO_{2003} - RO_{1995}) > 0$ & $RO_{2003} > 1$ and $RCA_{2003} < 1$ in two target markets—ASEAN and ASEAN+4.

The results of our analysis are presented in Table 3.14. The efficiency costs are lower for alignment with ASEAN relative to ASEAN+4 for all the economies except Japan. For China the cost of alignment with ASEAN is low relative to alignment with ASEAN+4 and lowest among the plus four economies. In comparison with about 67 per cent for ASEAN+4 only 26 per cent sectors are such that despite being comparatively disadvantageously placed in the world market China's exports from these sectors are getting increasingly oriented towards ASEAN. For India, in about 50 per cent of the sectors increased export orientation towards ASEAN is observed despite a lack of comparative advantage in the world market in comparison with 54 per cent such sectors in case of ASEAN+4. Corresponding figures for Korea are 68 and 78 per cent for ASEAN and ASEAN+4, respectively. Clearly, ASEAN+1 is a more cost-efficient arrangement for all the economies except Japan.[23]

Table 3.14

Efficiency Costs: Regional Orientation and Comparative Advantage*

	ASEAN	*ASEAN+4*
India	**50**	**53.6**
China	26.1	66.7
Japan	90.9	85.1
Korea	68.3	77.5

Note: * = % number of sectors.

23. As an alternative to this strict efficiency criterion if costs are calculated as percentage number of sectors that are increasingly getting oriented towards the target market-ASEAN or ASEAN+3 but experiencing a fall in comparative advantage in the world market, alignment with ASEAN implies lower cost and, hence, the more efficient option for all the plus four economies.

Alignment with ASEAN/ASEAN+4 vis-à-vis Multilateral Liberalisation

Alignment of Comparative Advantage

In this section we estimate the efficiency costs by undertaking a comparison of the comparative advantage of each of the plus four economies in the ASEAN+4/ASEAN market and the world market. Alignment of the structure of a country's comparative advantage in the two markets (ASEAN and world or ASEAN+4 and world) will imply fewer shifts in the production structure and lower costs as a consequence of an FTA with either ASEAN+4 or ASEAN. In addition, we have also compared the RCA across the three markets cross-classified by factor intensity. The analysis will provide evidence of a shift, if any, of the factors of production between industries that may be required as a consequence of regional integration. The efficiency costs as estimated in this section will also be indicative of the cost of participation in the regional FTA relative to participation in multilateral liberalisation which, according to conventional wisdom, is considered the 'first best' solution for attaining the potential benefits of a more open world economy.

The index of RCA has been calculated at HS 6-digit level for the most recent year of our sample period that is 2003.[24] The alignment of RCAs has been checked using the Spearman Rank Correlation Coefficient (SRCC) at the aggregate level (for all sectors) and separately for agriculture, manufacturing, minerals and fuels, chemicals and plastics, manufactures chiefly by materials and miscellaneous manufactures.[25] The SRCC, a non-parametric test, is often used to test for independence between two random variables. The range of possible values is from –1 to +1. A value close to +1/-1 will be interpreted to mean strong positive/negative rank correlation while a value of zero indicates a complete lack of correlation. For the purpose of our

24. As the arrangements are yet to fructify we calculate efficiency costs using the most recent year 2003 as indicative of future costs.

25. The alignment of the structure of comparative advantage has been undertaken irrespective of the value of the index. Alternately, alignment of only those commodities where countries are comparatively advantageously placed has also been tried. The results do not alter the earlier implications.

analysis, a high[26] rank correlation will be interpreted to mean the ranking of a country's industries by comparative advantage in a particular market, in this case, ASEAN or ASEAN+4 is similar to its ranking in the global market. A low coefficient will indicate that the ranking is considerably different across the two markets. The former implies lower cost of alignment with the respective preferential arrangement *vis-à-vis* the multilateral participation. The results are presented in Table 3.15.

The value of the SRCC is fairly high at the aggregate level and for individual sectors for all economies. As against multilateral liberalisation, participation in either of the two arrangements, that is, ASEAN+4 or ASEAN, does not imply significant shifts in the comparative advantage and, consequently, in the production structure. The extent of alignment is slightly higher at the aggregate level for all the economies for the ASEAN+4 market.

Table 3.15

Alignment of Comparative Advantage vis-à-vis Multilateral Liberalisation

	India	*China*	*Japan*	*Korea*
All Sectors	**0.66**	0.72	**0.73**	**0.63**
	0.73	(0.84)	***0.79***	***0.78***
Agriculture & Allied	**0.63**	0.60	**0.59**	**0.55**
	0.74	**(0.81)**	***0.67***	***0.74***
Manufacturing	**0.67**	**0.74**	**0.72**	**0.63**
	0.73	**(0.85)**	***0.78***	***0.78***
Minerals & Mineral Fuels	**0.64**	0.44	**0.68**	0.48
	0.82	**(0.85)**	**(0.89)**	***0.78***
Chemicals & Plastics	**0.70**	**0.75**	**0.65**	**0.67**
	0.75	**(0.86)**	***0.73***	**(0.82)**
Manufactures Chiefly by Materials	**0.69**	**0.74**	**0.71**	**0.61**
	0.74	**(0.83)**	***0.79***	***0.77***
Machinery	**0.55**	**0.72**	**0.76**	**0.65**
	0.57	***0.82***	**(0.84)**	***0.79***
Miscellaneous (HS 90-99)	0.38	**(0.85)**	**0.73**	**0.60**
	0.50	**(0.85)**	**(0.82)**	***0.75***

Note: Italicised: ASEAN+4; bold: moderate; Parenthesis: high; all others: low; all significant.

26. While no strict definitions are available we specify the range of 0-0.4 as low, 0.5-0.7 as modest and 0.8 and above as high for the SRCC.

Shifts in Factor Intensity

Five categories of factor intensity (FI) are identified. These are primary, unskilled-labour intensive, natural-resource intensive, human-capital intensive and technology intensive. The export patterns of the economies reclassified according to these five categories are compared for alignment across markets—world and ASEAN and world and ASEAN+4—using the SRCC. The results, presented in Table 3.16, are interesting. The value of the coefficient varies across countries but again falls in the range of being classified as modest to high, with very few in the latter category. India stands out as distinctly different from the other plus three economies. The export structure is aligned broadly similarly in ASEAN and world and ASEAN+4 and world for India. The value of the SRCC is almost the same in the two target markets. This implies an indifference between alignment with ASEAN or ASEAN+4 for India as neither implies any major shift of factors from their current employment in industries as oriented towards production for the global market. For the plus three economies ASEAN+4 is marginally more efficient than ASEAN.

Table 3.16

Alignment of Comparative Advantage and Shifts in Factor Intensity

	India	*China*	*Japan*	*Korea*
Human-capital Intensive	**0.71**	74	**0.72**	**0.65**
	0.75	(0.82)	***0.79***	***0.78***
Primary	**0.65**	**0.55**	**0.62**	**0.57**
	0.77	**(0.82)**	***0.77***	***0.79***
Unskilled-labour Intensive	**0.62**	**0.66**	**0.71**	**0.60**
	0.68	***0.75***	***0.78***	***0.75***
Natural-resource Intensive	**0.71**	**0.62**	**0.75**	**0.60**
	0.75	***0.77***	(0.80)	***0.77***
Technology Intensive	**0.64**	**0.72**	**0.71**	**0.66**
	0.67	(0.85)	***0.79***	(0.81)

Note: Italicised: ASEAN+4; bold: moderate; Parenthesis: high; all others: low; all significant.

Based on the above analysis of efficiency conditions it is considered that India's entry into the ASEAN+4 trade bloc will be more efficient if made through an ASEAN+1 arrangement. For China and Korea also the ASEAN+1 framework will be the more appropriate route. While the ASEAN+4 is marginally more efficient *vis-à-vis* multilateral liberalisation, costs of regional orientation of exports are lower for both Korea and China in an alignment with ASEAN in the ASEAN+1 arrangement. Alternative calculations of efficiency costs give a similar inference for Japan also. A convergence of the plus one initiatives of all the plus four economies with ASEAN may, therefore, be the more efficient route to achieving regional economic integration.

If ASEAN+1: Is There a First Mover Advantage?

If Asian economic integration is to be achieved through a convergence of the ASEAN+1 initiatives it is necessary that we analyse if a preemptive entry to ASEAN by any of the plus four economies will give it a first mover advantage *vis-à-vis* the other economies. Context and sequence of events is important in evaluating a preferential trading arrangement. The ASEAN-China FTA triggered a positive domino effect in the region. First, Japan followed suit by submitting a similar proposal and soon India and Korea also followed. The late entrants–Japan, India and Korea—may face export diversion on account of China being the first mover for FTA formation with ASEAN. This is particularly relevant as the Early Harvest Programme (EHP) of the ASEAN-China framework agreement is already in implementation and the FTA itself will be the first to be effective. In this section we examine if China's prior entry in ASEAN has an adverse impact through trade diversion on the other three economies. The degree to which each country is affected through trade diversion will depend critically on how much overlap there is between the exports of these countries.[27] Empirical analysis of the trade diversion effect of the ASEAN-China FTA on partners in the Asian FTA has not been undertaken so far. We undertake an analysis of the export similarity of the plus four economies by using conventional techniques and the

27. This exercise enables us to identify the trade diversion effects at the commodity level.

more innovative technique of evaluating the overlap of comparative advantage of the plus four economies at the sector and commodity levels.

Export Overlap

First, an evaluation of the degree of overlap of exports of the plus four economies has been undertaken by a simple analysis of export composition. The observations thus made are substantiated using the statistical technique of the SRCC. The SRCC is calculated for exports both at the 2 and 6-digit HS levels for India, China, Japan and Korea to ASEAN in 2003. As a check of the robustness of the results, the above exercise using correlations is repeated using a separate and equally popular export similarity technique known as the Finger–Kreinin Index (F-KI).[28]

The analysis of export composition reveals that there is very little similarity between the exports of India and the other three economies to ASEAN. At the 2-digit level (Table 3.17), we find that there is only a moderate export overlap between India and China, Korea and Japan. High overlap is indicated for exports of Korea with Japan. The export overlap between Korea and Japan is in fact the highest. The risk of trade diversion due to being left out or as a late entrant to the ASEAN would, therefore, not be particularly high for India. The risk of trade diversion is high for Korea *vis-a-vis* Japan. The results of the SRCC calculations at the 6-digit level of disaggregation presented in Table 3.18, however, allay the fears of trade diversion for all the four

---

28. The FKI estimates the export similarity by calculating the relative importance of various commodities in the export structure of pairs of countries and then using a filtering technique, that is,

$S = \sum i \min([Xia/\sum Xia],[\sum ib/\sum Xib])$

where

i =trade by disaggregated commodity.

a, b=two countries

The first ratio is the share of commodity I in country a's total exports and the second is the share of commodity i in country b's total exports. If these ratios are equal then the ratio in our formula would sum to one, indicating perfect similarity. On the other hand, if they are totally different, the formula would be zero. The index can thus range from 0 to 1.

Table 3.17

SRCC: Exports of the +4 Economies in ASEAN: 2003 (HS 2-digit)

	India	*China*	*Korea*	*Japan*
India	–	0.6	0.6	0.5
China	–	–	0.7	0.6
Korea Rep.	–	–	–	0.8
Japan	–	–	–	–

Table 3.18

SRCC: Exports of the +4 Economies in ASEAN: 2003 (HS 6-digit)

	India	*China*	*Korea*	*Japan*
India	–	0.4	0.3	0.2
China	–	–	0.4	0.4
Korea Rep.	–	–	–	0.5
Japan	–	–	–	–

economies. The value of SRCC is low and, therefore, indicative of a negligible export overlap between the plus four economies reinforcing further our conclusion that the risk of trade diversion for a late entrant is low as is the first mover advantage.

The F-K Index is estimated at the 2 and 6-digit level of disaggregation for India, China, Japan and Korea. The results are given in Tables 3.19 and 3.20. At the commodity level (HS 6-digit) the value of the index is small, thus corroborating the evidence on the SRCCs of the export structure of the plus four economies to ASEAN. The extent of competition between the plus three and India in the ASEAN market is almost non-existent.

As the scope for trade diversion on account of export similarity of the plus four economies to ASEAN+4 is almost negligible, the ASEAN+1 arrangement can be perceived as an efficient vehicle to achieve regional economic integration in Asia.

Table 3.19

Finger-Kreinin Index for the +4 Economies in ASEAN (HS 2-digit)

		India	*China*	*Japan*	*Korea*
India	1995	–	0.50	0.34	0.44
	2003	–	0.46	0.36	0.44
China	1995	0.50	–	0.50	0.58
	2003	0.46		0.67	0.71
Japan	1995	0.34	0.50	–	0.71
	2003	0.36	0.67	–	0.81
Korea	1995	0.44	0.58	0.71	–
	2003	0.44	0.71	0.81	–

Table 3.20

Finger-Kreinin Index for the +4 Economies in ASEAN (HS 6-digit)

		India	*China*	*Japan*	*Korea*
India	1995	–	0.24	0.15	0.15
	2003	–	0.27	0.16	0.18
China	1995	0.24	–	0.33	0.26
	2003	0.27	–	0.31	0.43
Japan	1995	0.15	0.33	–	0.27
	2003	0.16	0.31	–	0.46
Korea	1995	0.15	0.26	0.27	–
	2003	0.18	0.43	0.46	–

Overlap of Comparative Advantage

For greater robustness of our results we also examine the extent of overlap in comparative advantage that each economy enjoys in the ASEAN market. Among the plus four economies maximum overlap of comparative advantage in the ASEAN market is observed between India and China. For 52 per cent of the commodities where India and China have an advantage in the world market as well as in ASEAN, India enjoys greater comparative advantage relative to China in the ASEAN market. Indian exports of these commodities are likely to be adversely affected if China makes a prior entry in ASEAN. Trade will be diverted away from India. Further, for 72 per cent of these commodities, India is actually more competitive than China even in the world market.

Among these are commodities like marine products (fish and mollusks) and leguminous vegetables that belong to sectors 1-8 (HS classification).[29] Tariff concessions have been offered on these commodities under the EHP of China's FTA with ASEAN. India is, therefore, negatively affected through trade diversion on account of the implementation of the EHP. In the longer run when the ASEAN-China FTA is fully implemented, the maximum number of products that are likely to suffer export diversion belongs to the cotton sector. Commodities like cotton sewing thread, plain weave cotton, cotton yarn, twill weave cotton and woven fabric of cotton may suffer maximum export diversion. The advantage that China may get on account of an FTA may render it cheaper for ASEAN to import these commodities from China, in which case there is trade diversion from India and, in addition, efficiency loss for ASEAN. This implies that there is a cost to staying out of the ASEAN arrangement for India on account of China's preemptive entry in ASEAN. For Japan and Korea, on the other hand, the extent of trade diversion is greater *vis-à-vis* each other's entry in ASEAN rather than with respect to China's entry in ASEAN.

Conclusions

This study establishes the strength of ASEAN+4 as a potential trade bloc in Asia on the basis of trends in intra-regional trade and an augmented gravity model. Evidence on India's increasing trade linkages with ASEAN+4 is used to justify India's inclusion in the regional trade bloc. Our analysis reveals that for all the plus four economies a prior alignment with ASEAN in the ASEAN+1 framework may be a more efficient or least cost path to entering the ASEAN+4 bloc. The costs of aligning with ASEAN in the plus one framework are lowest for China. Regionally oriented export patterns do not imply any significant costs of adjustment of the production structure or shift of factors of production away from those that are consistent with the orientation towards the global market. A convergence of the plus one initiatives is also the more practical path to the emergence of an ASEAN plus four regional bloc as, the ASEAN initiatives with China,

---

29. A complete list of products where India is comparatively more advantageously placed in both the world and ASEAN market is available from the author on request.

Japan, Korea and India are as yet within the framework of the ASEAN+1 agreements and ASEAN negotiates with each country separately. However, to ensure that the ASEAN+1 agreements can effectively contribute to the formation of a regional economic entity in Asia in future greater focus on harmonisation of the +1 agreements is required, say for example, with respect to rules of origin, that at present may be scattered and inconsistent with one another. Harmonisation and compatibility among the +1 agreements is possible as the elements of these agreements are still being negotiated.

Finally, India, among the plus four economies, will be the most adversely affected due to trade diversion as a consequence of China's preemptive entry into ASEAN. The EHP of the ASEAN-China FTA that offers tariff concessions on commodities of sectors 1-8 (HS) will have a negative impact on India. In the long run the ASEAN-China FTA may also limit India's export potential in ASEAN in product groups like textiles, manmade filaments and footwears and gaiters that are largely unskilled labour intensive commodities. It is imperative, therefore, that India should hasten its process of negotiations for an early conclusion of the India-ASEAN FTA.

References

Asian Development Bank (2005). *Asian Economic Cooperation and Integration in Asia: Progress, Prospects and Challenges*. Manila: Philippines.

Baldwin, Richard E. (2006). "Managing the Noodle Bowl: The Fragility of East Asian Regionalism", *mimeo*. Geneva: Graduate Institute of International Studies.

Batra, Amita (2006). "India's Global Trade Potential: The Gravity Model Approach", *Global Economic Review*, Vol. 35(3).

Drysdale, Peter (2001). "The East Asia Community: What Trade Arrangements Make Sense?", Presentation to the conference on *Asian Values and Japan's Options*, October University of Singapore.

Drysdale, Peter (1969). "Japan, Australia and New Zealand: The Prospects for Western Pacific Economic Integration", *Economic Record*, Vol. 45(111).

Drysdale, Peter and Ross Garnaut (1982). "Trade Intensities and the Analysis of Bilateral Trade Flows in a Many Country World: A Survey", *Hitotsubashi Journal of Economics*, Vol. 2(2).

Frankel, Jeffrey, Ernesto Stein and Shang-Jin Wei (1995). "Trading Blocs and the Americas: The Natural, the Unnatural and the Super-natural", *Journal of Development Economics*, Vol. 47.

Kawai, Masahiro (2004). "Regional Economic Integration and Cooperation in East Asia", *mimeo*.

Kojima, Kiyoshi (1964). "The Pattern of Trade Among Advanced Countries", *Hitotsubashi Journal of Economics*, Vol. 5(1).

Krugman, P. (1993). "Regionalism vs Multilateralism: Analytical Notes", in Jaime de Melo and Arvind Panagariya (eds.), *New Dimensions in Regional Integration*, CEPR.

Lee, Jong-Wha, Innwon Park and Kwanho Shin (2004). "Proliferating Regional Trade Arrangements: Why and Whither?", Presented in Washington University in St. Louise, October.

Mingqui, Xu (2003). "East Asian Economic Integration: China's Perspective and Policy", *Pacific Economic Papers* No. 341. Canberra: Australian National University.

Ng, Francis and Alexander Yeats (2003). "Major Trade Trends in East Asia: What are Their Implications for Regional Cooperation and Growth?", *Policy Research Working Paper* No. 3084, Washington DC: World Bank.

Petri, P. (1992). "The East Asian Trading Bloc: An Analytical History", *Working Paper* No. 315. Waltham, MA: Brandeis University.

Ramkishen, S. Rajan and Rahul Sen (2005). "The New Wave of Free Trade Agreements in Asia, with Particular Reference to ASEAN, People's Republic of China and India", in *Asian Economic Cooperation and Integration in Asia: Progress, Prospects and Challenges*. Manila, Philippines: Asian Development Bank.

Schiff, Maurice and L. Alan Winters (2003). *Regional Integration and Development*. Washington DC: World Bank.

Scollay, Robert and John P. Gilbert (2001). *New Regional Trading Arrangements in the Asia Pacific? Policy Analyses in International Economics*, Vol. 63. Washington DC: Institute for International Economics.

Soesastro, Hadi (2003). "An ASEAN Economic Community and ASEAN+3: How do They Fit Together?", *Pacific Economic Papers* No. 338. Canberra: Australian National University.

Summers, Lawrence (1991). "Regionalism and the World Trading System", Paper presented at a seminar for the Federal Reserve Bank of Kansas City.

Vollrath, Thomas L. (1991). "A Theoretical Evaluation of Alternative Trade Intensity Measures of Revealed Comparative Advantage", *Weltwirtschaftliches Archiv*, Vol. 127(2).

Wonnacott, Paul and Mark Lutz (1989). "Is There a Case for Free Trade Areas?" in Jeffrey J. Schott (ed.), *Free Trade Areas and U.S. Trade Policy*. Washington DC: Institute for International Economics.

Yamazawa, Ippei (2001). "Assessing a Japan-Korea Free Trade Agreement", *The Developing Economies*, Vol. 39(1).

Yeats, Alexander (1997). "Does Mercusor's Trade Performance Raise Concerns About the Effects of Regional Trade Arrangements?", *Policy Research Working Paper*, No. 1729. Washington DC: World Bank.

4

Asian Economic Integration

Perspectives from a Chinese Scholar

LU JIANREN

The Global Development of Regional Economic Integration

Since the 1990s, regional economic integration has become an unstoppable trend throughout the world. The most telling feature of this trend is the explosive expansion of regional trade agreements (RTAs) in the past fifteen years (Figure 4.1). According to the latest WTO data, the number of RTAs of all kinds (including those in implementation or to be signed) had reached almost 300 by the end of 2005. 250 have been notified to the WTO. Out of these 250 RTAs, 130 were notified after January 1995, most of which have been signed recently. So far 173 RTAs have been notified to the WTO and come into effect. It is assessed that there are still over 70 RTAs which have not been notified to the WTO but are about to come into effect.[1]

Eighty-four per cent of the RTAs which have been notified to the WTO and are currently in force are free trade agreements (FTAs), while the remaining 16 per cent are customs unions (CUs) or preferential trade agreements (PTAs).[2] FTAs, CUs and PTAs are necessary organisational forms of regional economic integration.[3]

According to basic theories of regional economic integration, the process of integration usually passes through the following several

1. *http//www.wto.org*
2. Calculations based on the list from the WTO. See "Regional Agreements Notified to the GATT/WTO and in the Force", *http//www.wto.org*
3. Regional trade agreements (RTAs) are sometimes called Regional integration agreements (RIAs). RIAs include not only trade, but also investment and economic cooperation, economic policies, and even political fields (Schiff and Winters, 2002). RIAs apparently represent the development of the new wave of RTAs.

stages: free trade areas, customs unions, common markets, and economic unions. One can point out that preferential free trade areas are a step towards free trade areas, and the final integration leads to political and economic unions.

Figure 4.1

Notified RTAs to the GATT/WTO (1958-2004) by Entry into Force

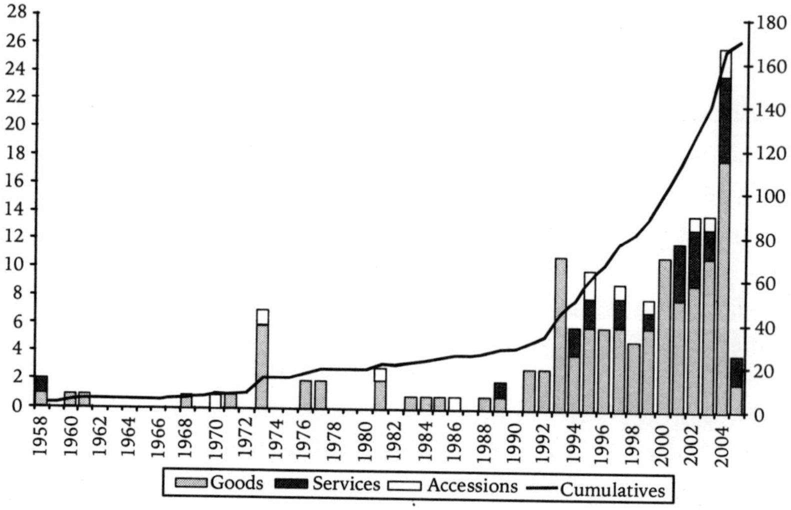

Source: Crawford and Fiorentino (2005). *http://www.wto.org*

The large-scale global expansion of RTAs has substantially changed the world trade structure. Although there still exists a global multilateral trade system—the WTO—the trade through RTAs has taken over 40 per cent of world trade (World Bank, 2000 Not in list of references). Almost all countries, whether a WTO member or not, are party to at least one RTA/FTA (World Bank, 2004). Going by present trends it is expected that the share of trade through RTAs will continue to increase.

This reflects the current accelerated development of economic regionalism. The new generation of RTAs/FTAs has broken through geographical limits.[4] Countries located at opposite ends of the globe,

4. The author has discussed the reasons why members of RTAs/FTAs are not limited to geographical boundaries in Lu (2003).

such as South Korea and Chile, can also sign a bilateral FTA. However, members of most RTAs/FTAs are still located within the same region or neighbouring regions. This shows that regional economic integration still follows certain patterns.

Figure 4.2

Organisational Forms and Stages of Development of Regional Economic Integration

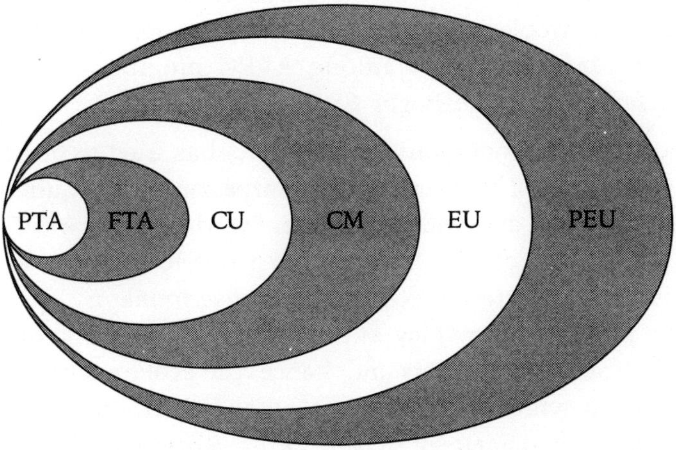

PTA = Preferential Trading Area	FTA = Free Trade Area
Cu = Customs Union	CM = Common Market
EU = Economic Union	PEU = Political Economic Union

Source: Adapted from Law, 2000. *http://www.fba.nus.sg*

The emergence of such a large number of RTAs/FTAs has caused wide concern among supporters of the WTO system. They think that these agreements undermine the multilateralism of the WTO. The global academia went through a debate to decide whether RTAs/FTAs would prove to be the building blocks or the stumbling blocks for the world trade system.[5] Currently, the majority of scholars thinks that as long as RTAs/FTAs are consistent with WTO rules, they will not be barriers to the world multilateral trade system but will promote the

5. Almost all studies on RTAs/FTAs mention this debate. For the latest work, see *World Bank* (2004).

global trade liberalisation and become supplementary to the multilateral system.

APEC, which aims at promoting trade liberalisation in the Asia-Pacific region, used to dismiss subregional agreements because it thought these small trade groups would impede the realisation of the Bogor Goals. However, faced with the increasing number of FTAs in the Asia-Pacific, APEC changed its attitude (Lu, 2003)—from acquiescence at the Shanghai Meeting in 2001 to encouragement at the Busan Meeting in 2005. In the Busan Declaration, APEC leaders stated that they would 'promote high-quality regional trade agreements and free trade agreements among APEC members, which were important avenues to the Bogor Goals' (APEC, 2005).

So far, the new generation of RTAs/FTAs has tried to be consistent with the WTO rules, with many even surpassing the requirements of the WTO in depth and width. In other words, they are 'WTO plus' (Lu, 2003). In spite of this, there are yet to be RTAs/FTAs with 'open regionalism'.[6] They are all exclusive and discriminatory against non-members. However, they play an important role in promoting trade liberalisation among members and, hence, the economic integration of the regions to which the members belong. With the backdrop of unsuccessful negotiations of the Doha Round and many other difficulties concerning the WTO system, RTAs/FTAs have become the real force behind regional trade liberalisation throughout the world. They signify the development of regional economic integration and, to some extent, accelerate economic globalisation.

Regional economic integration can bring all kinds of benefits to the involved parties. It has been defined as the status or process that helps member economies achieve economic benefits which they cannot achieve alone. This is done through cooperation or integration to utilise their comparative advantages in the pursuit of the shared

---

6. No RTAs of 'open regionalism' can solve the problem of 'freeriding' by non-members. Even APEC, which advocates open regionalism, would meet the same problem if it wished to promote trade liberalisation in a particular region. Therefore, it will be difficult for RTAs to become global public goods. This leads to the emergence of more RTAs because non-members are afraid of being discriminated against in trade. They have to either join that RTA or create their own.

objectives (Robson, 1990). Classic integration theories point out that economic integration brings about trade creation; enlarges the market capacity; creates economies of scale; stimulates competition and investment, facilitates the flow of factors of production, promotes international division of labour; enhances productivity and reduces transaction costs so that the resources are effectively allocated among the members, besides increasing the total welfare of all members after integration. The prospects of these benefits helped in the emergence of regional organisations for economic integration. Moreover, the examples shown by the European Union (EU) and NAFTA have had a great impact on the regional integration process in other parts of the world.

Current Situation of Asian Economic Integration

Compared to other regions of the world, Asia has been slow in responding to regional economic integration. The earliest such attempt might have been the Bangkok Agreement in 1975, with only five members: Bangladesh, India, Korea, Laos and Sri Lanka. China entered the agreement in 2000. But the Bangkok Agreement was only a preferential trade agreement that reduced tariffs. Because it has only a few members and covers a narrow area, it has only limited function in reducing tariff barriers among members.

Although ASEAN, established in 1976, is an important regional organisation in Asia, its contribution to real economic integration started only in the early 1990s. The ASEAN Free Trade Area (AFTA) was established in 1992 as a passive response to the challenges from European and North American economic integration organisations—EC and NAFTA—and did not look promising. However, AFTA has gradually developed into a standard subregional economic organisation and has propelled East Asian economic integration.

In South Asia, the South Asian Association for Regional Cooperation (SAARC) was set up in 1985, but its economic cooperation process is slow and at a low level. There was no substantial development in trade liberalisation in South Asia until the Agreement on SAARC Preferential Trading Arrangement (SAPTA) was signed in 1995.

In West Asia, the Gulf Cooperation Council (GCC) was established in 1981. Its members are six Middle East countries, including Saudi Arabia (Table 4.1). However, it is a comprehensive subregional cooperation organisation, having only recently adopted regional economic integration as one of its objectives.

In East Asia, economic integration started even later than in South Asia. Although the then Malaysian prime minister, Mahathir, called for the establishment of an East Asian Economic Group (EAEG) in 1990, it did not fructify because of opposition from the United States. Then ASEAN tried to push forward East Asian economic integration under the name of EAEC (East Asian Economic Caucus), but because of opposition from the United States and hesitation from Japan, this plan was not realised. Before the Asian financial crisis broke out in 1997, there was only one regional economic integration organisation—the AFTA—in East Asia (including North East Asia and South East Asia). None of the main economies, including Japan, South Korea, China, Taiwan and Hong Kong (their GDP ranked among the top 30 in the world in 1997), were party to any RTA/FTA, nor did they create their own.

There are several reasons why Asia has been slow to respond to economic integration. First, Asia is greatly diversified. It has a wide landscape and a huge population with 49 countries/areas. It is the most heterogeneous in the world in social and economic systems, economic development level, religion, culture and ethnicity. Such heterogeneity is not beneficial to economic integration.

Second, there was not enough momentum from within. Because of sustained economic backwardness in Asia, many underdeveloped agricultural countries were used to living a self-reliant life rather than developing foreign economic relations. Moreover, there was no close economic relationship either between the Asian countries or between the subregions. The East Asian economies with a lot of trade relations had most of their markets outside Asia. Such a situation made Asian countries slow to join the tide towards regional economic integration.

Third, there was an absence of core countries. Although there were many small wealthy countries in the Middle East, there were no truly developed countries in Asia except Japan. And, as a world big economy,

Japan had always cast its eyes globally and not solely on Asia. China and India, although they were the two most populous countries in Asia and in the world, did not pay much attention to regional economic integration till the 1990s. The experiences of the EU and NAFTA show that the role of core countries is indispensable to regional economic integration.

Fourth, the continent lacked the desired security environment. Asia had suffered war for long and there was still historical resentment between some of the big powers. The conflict between India and Pakistan was an important factor in the slow development of South Asian integration. Historical problems between China and Japan also influenced East Asian integration. Moreover, regional integration was difficult without resolving the Middle East problems and achieving peace in West Asia.

However, with the changes in international and regional conditions, such hurdles on the path to Asian economic integration were gradually ameliorated, and the momentum of the progress increased. Asian regional economic integration has achieved great progress since 1997 (Table 4.1).

First, the pace of regional economic cooperation and integration has accelerated. In early 1990, East Asia had conducted some functional regional cooperation, such as the joint development of the Tuman River valley. However, institutional regional cooperation started as a reaction to the shock from the Asian financial crisis in 1997. By this time most East Asian countries were already APEC members. APEC may be regarded as a 'quasi-institutional' form of regional cooperation (Lu, 2005). Some East Asian countries, including China, Japan and Korea, had gained experiences from APEC. China, particularly, had benefited from its experiences in APEC before entering the WTO. In December 1997, when East Asia was still suffering from the financial crisis, ASEAN, China, Japan and Korea held the first summit in Kuala Lumpur to discuss strategies to combat the crisis and work for regional cooperation. Since then an East Asian leaders' meeting has been held every year, developed from an informal to a formal mechanism and institutionalised into a 10+3 cooperation framework. Today it has become a whole set of mechanisms consisting of summits, ministerial meetings and high official meetings. Under the

10+3 framework, 17 areas for cooperation have been explored; 48 cooperation mechanisms have been established, including 14 ministerial ones, and over 100 cooperation projects. Members of 10+3 have made great achievements in areas of finance, agriculture, information, transportation and energy. The objective of the 10+3 cooperation is to establish an East Asian Free Trade Area, and further an East Asian Community. Without doubt, 10+3 has become the main channel to promote East Asian economic integration.

Table 4.1

FTA/EPA in Asia

Region	*Name of Agreement*	*Member*	*Status of Agreement*
South East Asia	AFTA	Old: Brunei, Malaysia, Philippines, Singapore, Thailand New: Cambodia, Laos, Myanmar, Vietnam	Agreement in force since 1993, zero tariffs for old members: 2015; new members: 2018
South East Asia and East Asia	ASEAN-China	ASEAN10 China	Agreement in force since 2004
	Singapore-China	Singapore China	Under negotiation within ASEAN-China FTA
	Thailand-China	Thailand China	Under negotiation within ASEAN-China FTA
	ASEAN-Japan	ASEAN 10 Japan	Agreement signed in 2003
	Japan-Singapore	Japan Singapore	Agreement in force since 2002
	Japan-Philippines	Japan the Philippines	Consultation concluded in 2004
	Japan-Thailand	Japan Thailand	Consultation concluded in 2005
	Japan-Malaysia	Japan Malaysia	Agreement signed in 2005
	Japan-Indonesia	Japan Indonesia	Agreement to be signed by the end of 2006

Contd...

...contd...

	Japan-Vietnam	Japan Vietnam	Start consultation since February 2006
	Japan-Brunei	Japan Brunei	Prepare official consultation in 2006
	ASEAN-Korea	ASEAN10 Korea	Agreement signed in 2005
	Korea-Singapore	Korea, Singapore	Under negotiation
	Korea-Thailand	Korea, Thailand	Under negotiation
North East Asia	Japan-Korea	Japan, Korea	Under negotiation
	China-Japan-Korea	China, Japan, Korea	Under study
South Asia	South Asian FTA(SAFTA)	Bhutan, Bangladesh India, Maldives, Nepal, Pakistan, Sri Lanka	Agreement signed in 2004 and in force since 2006
South Asia and South East Asia	India-ASEAN	India ASEAN10	Agreement signed in 2003, now under negotiation
	India-Thailand	India, Thailand	Agreement signed
	India-Singapore	India, Singapore	Under negotiation
	India-China	India, China	Under study
	BIMSTEC	Bangladesh, India, Myanmar, Sri Lanka, Thailand	Agreement signed in 2004, implemented within 10 years
	Pakistan-Singapore	Pakistan, Singapore	Proposed
	Sri Lanka-Singapore	Sri Lanka, Singapore	Under negotiation
Central Asia	Central Asian Economic Community	Kazakhstan, Azerbaijan, Kyrgyzstan, Uzbekistan	Agreement in force since 1999
Central Asia and East Asia	Shanghai Cooperation Organization (SCO)	China, Russia, Kazakhstan, Azerbaijan, Kyrgyzstan, Uzbekistan	Established in 2001, the SCO Multilateral Economic and Trade Cooperation Program signed in 2004
West Asia	Gulf Cooperation Council (GCC)	Bahrain, Kuwait, Qatar, Oman, Saudi Arabia and the United Arab Emirates	Established in 1981, The Gulf Common Market to be established in 2007
West Asia and East Asia	GCC-China	GCC6, China	Agreement signed in 2004, now under negotiation

Source: Gathered by the author.

At the same time, there are the 10+1 mechanisms, that is, the bilateral mechanisms of ASEAN+China, ASEAN+Japan and ASEAN+ Korea. So far, ASEAN has signed bilateral FTAs with each of the three countries. Besides, there is trilateral cooperation among China, Japan and Korea. In 2003, leaders of the three countries signed 'The Joint Declaration of China, Japan and South Korea on Promoting Tripartite Cooperation', which suggested establishing an FTA of the three countries in order to promote North East Asian economic integration.

Thus, four interconnected mechanisms of regional cooperation and integration have been formed in East Asia: ASEAN; ASEAN+1 (ASEAN-China, ASEAN-Japan, ASEAN-Korea); China-Japan-Korea; and ASEAN+3. Furthermore, many bilateral FTAs have been signed or are under negotiation among the countries in East Asia. An era of unprecedented regional integration has come for East Asia.

Second, the process of South Asian economic integration is going through ground-breaking developments. As mentioned above, South Asian countries signed SAPTA in 1995, and carried out some tariff reductions. The South Asian Summit in 1997 proposed to establish South Asian FTA in 2001. Because of India-Pakistan conflicts, that plan was shelved. Some bilateral agreements, however, made progress during this period. For example, India and Sri Lanka signed an FTA in 1998, which came into force in 2002. India also signed an FTA with Bangladesh and unilaterally offered preferential tariffs to Bhutan and Maldives. In 2003, India-Pakistan relations were ameliorated improving the prospect for bilateral economic relations. There was a good political environment for regional integration in South Asia. At the same time, the swift development of economic integration in East Asia stimulated South Asia. It was in such circumstances that, in January 2004, SAARC signed the South Asia Free Trade Agreement (SAFTA) which was set to be effective from January 2006 and reduce tariffs to 0~5 per cent in seven to ten years. (Lamberte, 2005). It is worth mentioning that SAFTA is a new generation of FTAs, which includes not only trade liberalisation but also trade facilitation, balance of payment, industrial security protection, trade disputes mechanisms and economic and technological assistance in its list of targets. The implementation of SAFTA will definitely accelerate the pace of South Asian economic integration.

Third, regional cooperation in Central Asia may be said to have achieved an unprecedented breakthrough. In the late 1980s, five Central Asian countries, namely Kazakhstan, Azerbaijan, Kyrgyzstan, Uzbekistan and Turkmenistan, became independent from the Soviet Union. The common features of the five countries are underdeveloped economy, state of transition from a centrally-planned economy to a market-economy and close economic relations with Russia and the opposite with other Asian regions. In order to reduce their economic dependence on Russia and increase their economic independence Kazakhstan, Azerbaijan, Kyrgyzstan and Uzbekistan formed the Central Asian Economic Community (Turkmenistan would not join any international organisation because of its commitment to remain neutral) and the process of Central Asian regional economic integration was begun. In 2000, the four countries signed development strategies for the integration and decided upon its four stages, that is, a free trade area, a customs union, a monetary union and a single labour market. They have made important progress in the first stage so far.

It should be noted that while pushing forward their own economic integration, Central Asian countries are trying to expand relations with other parts of Asia, particularly with East Asia whose economy is developing fast. The Shanghai Cooperation Organization (SCO), founded in 2001, has become the bridge for cooperation between Central Asia and China. The SCO is composed of the four Central Asian states, Russia and China. It was a security cooperation organisation at first, but is progressing towards economic cooperation as well. In September 2003 the SCO adopted a plan for multilateral economic and trade cooperation and identified its objectives. They include realising goods trade, services trade and investment liberalisation by 2020. In July 2005, India, Pakistan and Iran were accepted as observers. The SCO is likely to become an important organisation for Asian economic integration in the future.

Fourth, West Asia has also begun economic integration. As early as 1981, six Arab countries, namely, Bahrain, Kuwait, Oman, Qatar, Saudi Arabia and the United Arab Emirates (UAE), created the Gulf Cooperation Council (GCC). It is an important regional organisation in the Middle East, with the aim of strengthening coordination and cooperation between the member economies, helping each country develop industries, agriculture and technology and conducting joint projects. However, economic integration was not in its agenda for a long time. With the accelerated global and regional economic integration, especially in East Asia, West Asia has made promising progress too. On 1 January 2003, the six countries of the GCC launched customs union, which eliminates tariff between members and adopts 5 per cent tariff to imports from non-members. The GCC also decided upon a time frame for Gulf economic integration, that is, to form a Gulf Common Market by the end of 2007, and to issue a common currency in January, 2010.[7] Because of their similar high levels of economic development, which is a sound basis for integration, the GCC is likely to develop fast (by adopting a common currency) into a regional economic integration organisation in Asia.

Finally, inter subregional economic integration has emerged in Asia. Economic integration is not only accelerating within subregions of East Asia, South Asia and West Asia, but also seems to be expanding into cooperation between the subregions. The most noticeable is the gradual merging between East Asia and South Asia. The most active players in the two regions—ASEAN and India—signed a bilateral FTA in 2003. This marked the beginning of the economic integration of East and South Asia. The two biggest Asian countries, China and India, have started talks over an FTA, which would be the most populous bilateral FTA in the world. Moreover, India, Pakistan and Sri Lanka are talking about bilateral FTAs with Singapore and Thailand (Table 4.1). All these have promoted the economic integration of South, East and South East Asia, and of Asia as a whole.

The reasons why Asian economic integration has accumulated such momentum in recent years include external ones, such as the difficulties with the multilateral trade system and the burgeoning of regional organisations elsewhere. There are also two internal reasons. First, the share of intra-regional trade has been increasing in Asia with its fast economic development. The close economic relations make conditions increasingly mature for economic integration. Second, with

---

7. *http: //www.xinhuanet.com*

its continuing fast economic development, China has become the engine for Asian economic growth, and propelled the increase of trade and investment in Asia. Many Asian countries, hoping to ride piggy-back on China's economic growth, ask to expand economic cooperation with China. It was under such circumstances that the China-ASEAN FTA (CAFTA) was initiated following a proposal from China. CAFTA is playing a positive role in promoting East Asian and Asian regional economic integration. This benchmarks the entry of Asia into a new era of economic integration.

Economic Integration Strategies of Asian Countries

Currently the most active proponents for Asian economic integration are ASEAN, China, Japan, Korea and India. In the following section we will briefly analyse their strategies in this regard.

ASEAN's 'Concentric' Strategy

ASEAN was the first to practise regional economic integration in Asia. From the earliest AFTA, to today's ASEAN+3 and several ASEAN+1 mechanisms, ASEAN has been leading the process of East Asian economic integration. Fundamentally, ASEAN's momentum comes from the needs of the member countries. It is an association of middle to small or weak countries, and economic integration is their only choice for survival and development, and for combating external threats. It is the strong internal momentum that has pushed ASEAN into carrying out the AFTA plans and making it successful. At the same time, ASEAN has realised that AFTA is a kind of south-south integration, but theory and practice of economic integration have shown that such a system of cooperation cannot compete with north-south integration.[8] Since in organisations of south-south integration the internal markets are usually smaller than north-south ones and the share of intra-regional trade is not high it is more difficult to form close division of labour and to coordinate integration policies. There is also severe trade diversion. Most of these 'born defects' exist with AFTA. For instance, intra-regional

8. The rules of regionalisation point out that north-south agreements are better than south-south agreements in that 'RIAs with high-income countries would bring more economic benefits than with poor countries' (Schift and Winters, 2002).

trade lingers around 20 per cent of total AFTA trade. In 2002 AFTA's intra-regional trade was 22.8 per cent while that of NAFTA was 56 per cent and that of the EU 61 per cent.

ASEAN hopes its more developed neighbours will help it to overcome the defects of south-south integration. It has cast its eyes on Japan, China and Korea in North East Asia. Japan is the second largest economy in the world and the most developed country in Asia, and has long-term close economic relations with ASEAN. China is the fastest growing big economy in the world, and maintains relations of cooperation with ASEAN. Korea is a newly industrialised country, and is progressing towards joining the ranks of developed countries. Of course, ASEAN realised that it was unrealistic to ask the three countries to directly join AFTA. However, it was possible to expand the scope of cooperation and establish bilateral and multilateral FTAs with them with the core of AFTA. Only when the size was enlarged could ASEAN benefit from north-south integration.

With sophisticated and prudent strategies, ASEAN won the trust from big countries because its political and economic positions are unthreatening, it has experiences in regional integration, and it had obtained the leading power in East Asian economic integration. (Lu, 2006a). At this stage, ASEAN adopts a 'concentric' strategy. The core is the 'ASEAN Community'.[9]

The first circle consists of several 10+1 mechanisms including those with China, Japan, Korea, India, Russia and Australia. The second circle is 10+3. And the East Asia Summit (10+3+Australia, New Zealand, India and Russia) is the third circle (Figure 4.3). Apparently, ASEAN wants to dominate not only East Asian economic integration, but also Asia and Asia-Pacific integration.

This strategic map of ASEAN will probably become the blueprint for the future 'East Asia Community', or even 'Pan-Asia

9. The 'ASEAN Community' is a grand objective raised by ASEAN in 2003, which would be made of three pillars: ASEAN Economic Community, ASEAN Security Community and ASEAN Social and Cultural Community. ASEAN would realise comprehensive integration in the form of community. The time frame was set to be 2020, and later changed to 2015. But the Community is currently just a blueprint without details.

Community'.[10] ASEAN has been pushed onto the driver's seat of the East Asian and Asian regional economic integration wagon, and will play a leading role for a long period. Considering the circumstances in East Asia and Asia, that is an appropriate choice from every aspect.

Figure 4.3

ASEAN's 'Concentric' Strategy

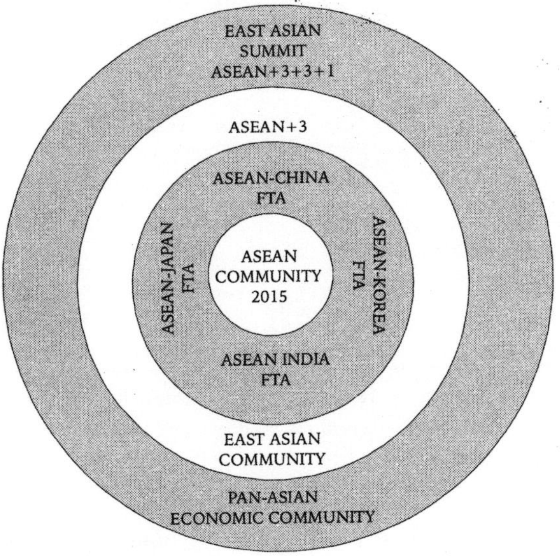

Source: Created by the author.

China's 'Big Periphery' Regional Cooperation Policy

China is located in East Asia and Asia Pacific. Its foreign trade and economic relations are mainly in Asia Pacific, particularly its 'big periphery' which includes Russia of North Asia, Japan and Korea of North East Asia, Hong Kong and Taiwan of East Asia, countries of South East Asia, South Asia, Central Asia and Australia of South Pacific.

In 2005, for example, seven of the top ten trade partners of China came from the 'big periphery', and occupied 50 per cent of China's total trade (Table 4.2). If India, the five countries of Central Asia and New Zealand are added, they take almost 60 per cent. This high level was maintained for the five years from 2001 to 2005 (Table 4.3).

10. 'Pan' usually means the whole region. Here it refers to the wider region of Asia, including not only Asian countries but also Australia, New Zealand and Russia.

Table 4.2

China's Top 10 Trade Partners in 2005

(US$ Billion)

Rank	Country/Area	Value	Share (%)
1	EU	217.3	15.3
2	USA	211.6	14.9
3	Japan	184.4	13.0
4	Hong Kong	136.7	9.6
5	ASEAN	130.4	9.2
6	Korea	111.9	7.9
7	Taiwan	91.2	6.4
8	Russia	29.1	2.0
9	Australia	27.3	1.9
10	Canada	19.2	1.3
	Top 10 Partners	1159.1	81.5
	7 of Top 10*	**711.0**	**50.0**
	Others	263.0	18.5
	Total	1422.1	100.0

Note: * = Japan, Hong Kong, ASEAN, Korea, Taiwan, Russia, Australia.
Source: Ministry of Commerce, People's Republic of China (PRC)

Table 4.3

Share of Asian and Selected Partners in China's Trade, 2001-2005

(Per Cent)

Partners	2001	2002	2003	2004	2005
Japan	17.2	16.4	16.0	14.5	13.0
ASEAN	8.2	8.8	9.2	9.2	9.2
Hong Kong	11.0	11.1	10.3	9.8	9.6
Korea	7.0	7.1	7.4	7.8	7.8
Taiwan Province	7.1	7.2	6.9	6.8	6.4
Russia	2.1	1.9	1.9	1.8	2.0
Australia	1.7	1.7	1.6	1.8	1.9
India	0.7	0.8	0.9	1.2	1.3
South Asia*	0.5	0.5	0.5	0.5	0.6
Central Asia	0.3	0.4	0.5	0.5	0.6
New Zealand	0.2	0.2	0.2	0.2	0.2
Asia	56.5	58.1	58.2	57.6	56.8
Asia+3**	60.6	61.9	61.9	61.4	60.9

Note: * = excluding India
** = Asia plus Russia, Australia and New Zealand.
Source: Ministry of Commerce, PRC.

In the past 20 years, the development of China's foreign trade has been mostly led by foreign direct investments (FDI), most of which have come from the 'big periphery', especially Japan, Korea, Hong Kong, Taiwan and Singapore. FDI from Europe and the United States has increased substantially in recent years. With China's increasingly closer trade and economic relations with countries and regions in the 'big periphery', their economic interdependence has deepened as well. This provides a positive condition for China's economic integration with its 'big periphery'. So, naturally, the 'big periphery' strategy has become important for China's intention to pursue regional economic integration.

Furthermore, because it was excluded from GATT/WTO for a long time and could not enjoy the benefits from the multilateral trade system, China puts emphasis on strengthening economic and trade cooperation with neighbouring countries and regions. Among economies in the 'big periphery', China has the closest economic relationship with those in East Asia. China has realised very early that only if the whole of East Asia forms a close integration can all the members of East Asia develop well and the Chinese economy have the foundation for its own development in the future. Therefore, China has been supportive of East Asian regional economic integration. In end-1990 when Mahathir had proposed the establishment of an 'East Asian Economic Group' China had supported this idea. However, China's focus then was on its entry into the WTO, and it lacked experience of regional economic cooperation. Not until China joined APEC in 1991 did it start to accumulate such experience, and this helped it to prepare for participation in all kinds of regional economic integration.

Since the start of the 10+3 mechanism, China has been actively participating in East Asian cooperation. It has come up with many suggestions which have contributed to East Asian integration. China supports an East Asian Community as the long-term goal of 10+3, the initiative taken by ASEAN for an 'East Asian Summit', and ASEAN's leading role in East Asian cooperation. The signing of an FTA between China and ASEAN has directly propelled Japan, Korea, India, Australia and New Zealand to sign FTAs with China, which promoted the integration process of East Asia and Pan-Asia.

Of course, besides the 'big periphery' policy, China also considers other factors in its regional economic integration strategy. They include the need to expand international markets, obtain resources and raw materials, and coordinate with its foreign policy. East Asia and the 'big periphery' are China's traditional markets, but it also needs access to developed markets in Europe and the United States, and to new markets in Africa and Latin America. This requires China to cooperate and integrate with them. The denial by the EU and the United States of China's market economy status has become the main obstacle in its access to European and American markets. Sooner or later, however, China will obtain the market economy status because the long-term costs of the EU and the United States will surpass the short-term benefits if they do not cooperate with China as major trade economies in the world.

China is currently consulting with over 20 countries or regions about FTAs, some of which have been signed. If we analyse the locations of the partners, there is a basic strategy of 'approaching the big periphery, big or new markets, and energy and important resources'. For instance, China's FTAs with Chile, South Africa Customs Union, and India show the strategy of approaching new markets, while the ones with the GCC, SCO, ASEAN, Australia and New Zealand are for energy and important resources. Most of these countries are in geographical proximity with China (Table 4.4).

In summary, with the China-ASEAN FTA as a starting point, China has entered a period of actively establishing FTAs with countries in Asia and the 'big periphery' and has become an enthusiastic proponent of East Asian and Asian regional economic integration.

Japan's 'Expanded East Asian Community' Strategy

Although Japan was the first country in Asia to propose regional economic cooperation,[11] the Japanese government has preferred the multilateral trade system and dismissed regional trade agreements.[12]

11. As early as the 1960s, there were some non-governmental proposals from Japan for establishing an 'Organization of Asia Economic Cooperation' (OAEC), and a 'Pacific Free Trade Area' (PAFTA).

12. For the reasons for Japan's objection to RTAs/FTAs, see Lu (2006b).

However, after Korea and Mexico proposed Japan to establish FTA in 1998, Japan's trade policy started to change from multilateralism to selective bilateralism and Singapore's proposal of an FTA in 1999 facilitated that change. The reasons had to do with the obstacles faced by the WTO and APEC, as well as Japan's adjustment of trade policies to get out of ten years' recession. (Lu, 2006b)

Table 4.4

Overview of China's Participation in Regional Cooperation Organisations

Category	*Name*	*Information*
Non-institutional organisations	Asia-Europe Meeting (ASEM), established in 1996. China is a founding member.	Members include 25 EU countries, 10 ASEAN countries, China, Japan, Korea, and the European Commission. It is mainly for political dialogues, but also for some economic and trade cooperation. The Summit is held once very two years.
	Shanghai Cooperation Organization, established in 2001.	Members include China, Russia, Kazakhstan, Kyrgyzstan, Tajikistan and Uzbekistan. Its predecessor was the Shanghai Five Countries in 1996, now becoming a political, security and economic cooperation organisation. The Summit is held once a year.
Quasi-institutional organisations	Asia-Pacific Economic Cooperation (APEC), established in 1989. China joined in 1991 together with Hong Kong, China and Chinese Taipei.	Members include the US, Canada, Australia, New Zealand, Mexico, Chile, Peru, China, Hong Kong, China, Chinese Taipei, Japan, Korea, Papua New Guinea, Malaysia, Thailand, the Philippines, Singapore, Brunei, Vietnam, and Russia. The Bogor Goals were set up in 1994, aimed at realising trade and investment liberalisation of developed/ developing members in 2010/ 2020. It holds annual summits.
	10+3 (ASEAN plus 3), established in 1997. China is a founding member.	Members include 10 ASEAN countries, China, Japan and Korea. It holds annual leaders' meetings. It promotes economic,

Contd...

...Contd. ...

Category	*Name*	*Information*
		political and security cooperation. The Summit is held once a year. In May 2000 the Chiang Mai Initiative was adopted.
	10+1 (ASEAN plus 1, started in 1997)	A bilateral cooperation mechanism between China and ASEAN. It adopted a Plan of Action in 2004, involving economic political and security aspects. It holds its annual summit at about the same time as that of the 10+3.
Institutional organisations	The Bangkok Agreement, signed in 1975. China joined in 2001.	Members include India, Bangladesh, Sri Lanka, Laos, Korea, the Philippines and China. It is a preferential trade agreement, which has increased the scope of tariff reduction since 2006.
	China-ASEAN Free Trade Area (CAFTA)	The Framework Agreement on China-ASEAN Comprehensive Economic Cooperation was signed in November 2002. The Early Harvest Programme came into force in January 2004, and comprehensive tariff reduction was started in July 2005. It will be realised within 2015.
	China-Thailand Zero Tariff Fruit and Vegetable Agreement	It was signed under the Frame work Agreement on China-ASEAN Comprehensive Economic Cooperation in June 2003, and took effect in October 2003.
	The Closer Economic Partnership Arrangement between China and Hong Kong (CEPA)	It was signed in 2003 and started implementation in January 2004, including trade of goods and services, and trade and investment liberalisation.
	The Closer Economic Partnership Arrangement between China and Macao (CEPA)	It was signed in 2003 and started implementation in January 2004, including trade of goods and services, and trade and investment liberalisation.
Institutional organisations	Free Trade Area between China and the Southern African Customs Union (SACU)	Members include China, Botswana, Lesotho, Namibia, South Africa and Swaziland. Negotiations were launched in June 2004.

Contd...

...Contd. ...

Category	*Name*	*Information*
	China-Gulf Cooperation Council Free Trade Area	Members are China, Bahrain, Kuwait, Oman, Qatar and the United Arab Emirates. The Framework Agreement on Economic, Trade, Investment and Technological Cooperation was signed in 2004 and is now under negotiation.
	China-Chile FTA	Negotiation was started in 2004.
	China-New Zealand FTA	Negotiation was started in 2004.
	China-Australia FTA	Negotiation was started in 2005.
	China-Pakistan FTA	It was signed in 2005 and started to implement the Early Harvest Programme.
	China-India FTA	The feasibility study started in 2005.
	China-Japan-Korea FTA	The Joint Declaration to Promote Cooperation among China, Japan and Korea was signed in 2003 and started feasibility study.

Source: Gathered by the author.

In January 2002, the signing of the 'Agreement between the Republic of Singapore and Japan for a New Age Economic Partnership' (JSEPA) signified the incipience of Japan's 'selective bilateralism'. Shortly afterwards, the Japanese government published the white paper which designed the four stages of Japan's FTA strategy in Asia. First, it would sign bilateral FTAs with Korea, Thailand, Malaysia, the Philippines and Indonesia (four old members of ASEAN; Japan has signed with Singapore). Second, it would sign FTAs with new members of ASEAN to complete an FTA with ASEAN as a whole. Third, China would be accepted to the hubs of the Japan-Korea FTA and the Japan-ASEAN FTA. And, finally, as regards Taiwan Province and Hong Kong, China would be accepted to 'realise wider East Asian integration'.[13]

The rapid development of the China–ASEAN FTA process and its impact on the region put pressure on Japan to accelerate its own FTA process in East Asia. From the end of 2004 to the beginning of 2006, Japan has signed an FTA with Malaysia, concluded consultations with

13. Japan's FTA Strategy, *http//www.mofa.go jp*

the Philippines and Thailand, started consultation with Vietnam and Brunei and is preparing to sign an FTA with Indonesia (Table 4.1). A middle-turn programme on FTAs has been developed by the Japanese government, in which FTAs will be signed with 15 countries/areas around the world by 2010 and those who have rich resources or market potentials will be given priority in the programme.[14]

Furthermore, Japan proposed a regional integration strategy of an 'Expanded East Asia Community'. An 'East Asian Community' was first proposed by the East Asian Vision Group (EAVG) in 2001 as the long-term goal of East Asian cooperation, and Japan responded promptly to that. In January 2002, the Japanese prime minister, Koizumi, proposed the Japanese version of an 'East Asian Community.' Its difference from the EAVG's version is that Australia and New Zealand were to be included besides 10+3. Japan's reasons to include them were, first, to appease the United States for its dissatisfaction about East Asian integration and the two, being American allies, could be its representatives for resolving the issue; and, second, to solidify Japan's leading position in East Asian integration. Japan thought that Australia and New Zealand shared common qualities with Japan and could expand Japan's team in the Community.

At the East Asian Summit in December 2005, Japan attempted to discuss expanding 'East Asia Community', and proposed to adopt 'freedom, democracy and human rights' as its value system. However, Japan's proposal was not realised. Both ASEAN and China wanted to build the 'East Asia Community' within the 10+3 framework. Neither was Japan's proposed value system adopted.

An overview of Japan's Asian regional integration strategy reveals several interesting points. First, while choosing FTA partners, Japan puts Singapore first and China the last. The claimed reason is 'first easy ones and then difficult ones', but the real motivation is to ensure Japan's leading position in East Asian economic integration, so that it would not fall into the hands of China. Second, Japan's agricultural liberalisation is always a political obstacle, which would prohibit it from signing FTAs with other Asian countries. Even if FTAs were

---

14. "Japan hopes to have 15 FTAs by 2010", *http://www.channelnewsasia.com*, 5 February, 2006.

signed, they would not have a high quality if a lot of agricultural products were excluded. Besides, labour service market entry is another obstacle in Japan's path to implementing its FTA strategy. Japan does not want to open its labour service market. That is the reason why Japan has not signed FTAs/CEPAs with the Philippines and Thailand until now. Third, Japan has a weak Asian consciousness and relies heavily on the United States on diplomacy and security issues. This makes its Asian integration policy hesitant and uncertain. Finally, considerations of how to deal with historic problems and improve relations with Asian countries, especially Korea and China, would directly influence the progress of East Asian economic integration.

Korea's 'Era of North East Asia' Strategy

Because of its small domestic market, Korea has been relying on international markets for economic development. The Asian financial crisis in 1997 hit Korean *chaebols'* global expansion and made them turn to East Asia. In fact, Korea was the first country to officially propose 'East Asian economic' integration. At the 10+3 Summit in 2000 the then Korean president, Kim Dae-jung, suggested for the first time the setting up of an 'East Asian Economic Community'. The EAVG was formed under his proposal as well. Korea is also actively promoting North East Asian economic integration, aiming at a 'North East Asian Economic Community' consisting of Korea, Japan and China.

After Roh Moo-hyun took up the reins of presidency, he pursued the idea of the 'Era of North East Asia' more explicitly. The boost to this idea came from the belief that Korea was the centre of North East Asia, with a world-class information infrastructure, an outstanding reserve of human resource and distinguished creativity. Korea would be the logistics and financial centre of North East Asia, which would become a 'community of prosperity'.

In order to achieve the dream of an 'Era of North East Asia' Korea made the 'North East Asian strategies', which were, first, to establish a Korea-China-Japan FTA; second, to construct peace mechanisms in the Korean Peninsula; and, third, to make Korea the 'hub' of North East Asian economy, that is, the logistics and financial centre.[15]

15. *Dynamic Korea*, No. 3 (Weekly) (2003) Korean Embassy in China.

It should be mentioned that when Korea made the judgment that the twenty-first century would become a 'North East Asian Era', it predicted China's role optimistically. It thought that China would surpass the United States by around 2020 to become the biggest economy in the world, and so then there would come an 'East Asian Era'. That would be a strong foundation for the 'Era of North East Asia'.[16]

Although Korea is ambitious about the creation of the 'North East Asian Era', it is very cautious in its involvement in East Asian integration. Korea did not start negotiating FTAs with ASEAN until January 2005, and the one with Japan is lagging behind. It may also be mentioned here that Korea has not started negotiations with China. One reason the Korea-Japan-China FTA proposed by Korea has yet to enter the negotiation stage is that it is difficult for Korea to liberalise its agricultural sector. In this respect, Korea has the same problem as Japan.

India's 'JACIK' Strategy

In the early 1990s, India came up with a 'Look East' policy, which was initially to expand its boundaries for economic development through the East Asian economic boom, and to strengthen its economic connection with East Asia so as to push forward domestic economic reforms. As a big Asian country, India did not participate in any regional cooperation except that of South Asia. Its request to join APEC was turned down. This made India turn to East Asia, in the hope of becoming a part of the East Asian integration, and to form a wider 'Asian Economic Community'.

The former Indian prime minister, Atal Behari Vajpayee, was the first to propose an 'Asian Economic Community' (AEC). The present prime minister, Manmohan Singh, formally raised this idea before East Asian countries. The purpose behind an 'Asian Economic Community' is actually to turn East Asian 10+3 into 10+4 by including India. Indian scholars created the acronym, JACIK, from the names of the 14 countries, that is, Japan, ASEAN, China, India and Korea (Kumar, 2005).

16. See *National Economist Association*, No.3 (2003) Seoul.

The population in JACIK is over 3 billion—half of the world's population. Its trade volume is higher than that of NAFTA, and its foreign reserve is more than the total of NAFTA and the EU (Table 4.5). It has definitely the power to equal the EU and NAFTA. Because JACIK would mainly include developing countries, it would change the unfair international economic balance dominated at present by developed countries.

Table 4.5

Size of Existing and Proposed Regional Economic Blocs, 2003

Parameter	*EU*	*NAFTA*	*ASEAN*	*ASEAN+3*	*JACIK*
GDP (US$ trillion)	10.069	11.716	0.672	7.014	7.613
Per cent to world total	27.69	32.23	1.85	19.29	20.94
GNI (US$ trillion)	10.132	11.855	2.095	13.030	16.098
Per cent to world total	19.75	23.10	4.08	25.39	31.37
Exports (US$ trillion)	2.603	0.996	0.447	1.552	1.607
Per cent to world total	34.80	13.32	5.98	20.75	21.48
International reserves (US$ trillion)	0.545	0.206	0.244	1.516	1.618
Population (billion)	0.418	0.323	0.537	2.001	3.065
Per cent to world total	6.66	5.15	8.56	31.91	48.87

Note: GNI = gross national income; GDP = gross domestic product.
Source: Lamberte, 2005.

In order to carry out the strategy for an AEC, India has been making efforts to strengthen economic and trade relations with East Asian countries. India took the initiative to sign an FTA with ASEAN in 2003. Its relationship with China has been enhanced, with bilateral trade growing fast and an FTA under discussion. Its trade and economic relations with Japan and Korea have been largely promoted, particularly with the increase of their investments into India.

India incentive to propel an AEC is threefold: first, to improve its disadvantaged position in the global regional economic integration race; second, to ride on the fast train of economic growth in East Asia and China and share its benefits ; and third, to march into the world from East Asia and turn itself from an Asian power into a global power.

Whatever India's intentions are, from an objective perspective, it would be mutually beneficial if India becomes a participant in the East Asian integration. India is in a stage of fast and continuing economic growth, and will become one of the biggest economies in the world. Among the JACIK countries, India has the youngest population and thus the biggest potential of labour resources. India's economic structure is complementary with that of East Asia. The advantages of a link-up between India's software industry and China's manufacturing industry would enhance JACIK's share of world exports. Besides, although the per capita income of India is low, the middle class is increasing and will provide a huge consumer market for East Asian economies. India could obtain more FDIs and advanced technologies from East Asian economies and enhance its international competitiveness. According to studies by Indian scholars, the gains can reach a level equivalent to 3 per cent of the combined GDP of JACIK economies if a regional trading arrangement is combined with investment liberalisation and mobility in skilled labour (Lamberte, 2005 and Kumar, 2005). Apparently, all members of JACIK would benefit.

A Blueprint of Pan-Asian Economic Community

Soon after India began advocating for the AEC a blueprint for a wider regional integration was revealed—a Pan-Asian Economic Community. In December 2005, 16 countries held the first East Asian Summit (EAS). They included the 13 East Asian countries and India, Australia and New Zealand. The decision to hold the EAS had been made earlier at the 10+3 Summit in 2004. The original plan had been to discuss the establishment of an East Asian Community. Immediately after they heard that news, India, Australia, New Zealand, Russia, Mongolia and Pakistan all requested to participate in the EAS. ASEAN then accepted India, Australia and New Zealand to the Summit with Russia as an observer, based on three conditions: the country should be a dialogue partner of ASEAN, should have signed the 'Treaty of Amity and Cooperation in South East Asia'(TAC), and should have substantial relations with ASEAN. Although the first EAS did not formally include the East Asian Community as a topic for discussion, these newcomers apparently entered in order to be a part of the East Asian integration process. This shows that the influence of East Asian economic integration has not only expanded to South Asia, but far beyond Asia. The name 'East Asia Summit' has already become incompatible with its substance, and it should probably be renamed as the 'Pan-Asian Summit'. If the members in the EAS form a community, its scale and global influence would be beyond those of JACIK, which would be a 'Pan-Asian Economic Community' (Figure 4.4 and Table 4.6).

Figure 4.4

A Blueprint of Pan-Asian Economic Community

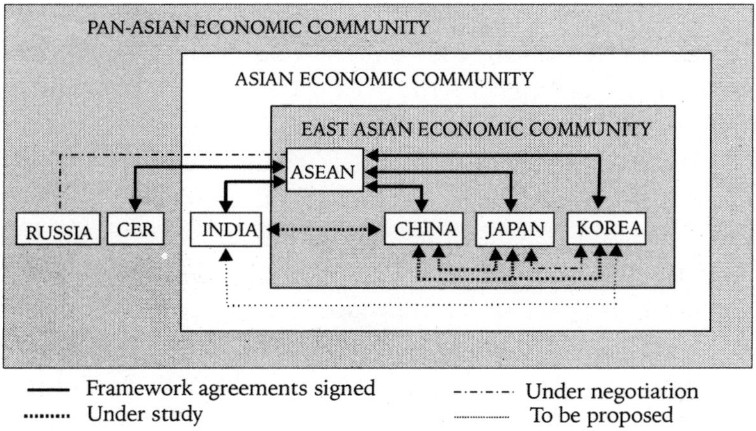

Source: Created by author.

Table 4.6

GDP Scale of East Asian Summit Members in 2003

Country	*GDP (US$ billion)*	*Country*	*GDP (US$ billion)*
Japan	4299.73	Philippines	79.27
China	1416.75	Vietnam	39.02
Korea	605.54	Myanmar	9.61
India	570.76	Brunei	4.72
Australia	511.95	Cambodia	4.21
Russia	431.43	Laos	2.04
Indonesia	208.63	**Total**	**8522.06**
Thailand	143.30	EU	10069.00
Malaysia	103.74	USA	10971.20
Singapore	91.36	World	36327.44

Source: World Bank.

The Pan-Asian Economic Community is imagined as an institutional arrangement, consisting of some neighbouring Asian countries and countries that have close economic, political, cultural and geographical relations with them—Russia, Australia and New Zealand. Besides current members of the EAS, Mongolia, North Korea and Pakistan would be considered as well. The Pan-Asian Economic Community would be an expanded AEC. Its short-term goal would be to establish a Pan-Asian FTA, abolish tariff and quota among members, and then establish a Customs Union. Its long-term goal would be to establish an economic community of free mobility of capital and labour, and to make common trade and industrial policies.

The welfare brought by the Pan-Asian Economic Community would be far higher than that of the AEC. The participation of Russia, Australia and New Zealand would largely enhance the power and quality of the community. Russia is a big country of energy and resources, and Australia and New Zealand are developed countries. Their participation would increase the share of the north in the community, enhance the economic structure and factor complementarity among members. The Pan-Asian Economic Community holds two-thirds of the world's population and encompasses one-third of the world's geographical size. It would have more natural resources and economic scale than the EU and NAFTA and become 'incomparable' in regional economic integration in the world.

Indeed, that is just a wishful blueprint. There is a long way to go before it is realised. Many obstacles stand in the way of integration, including uneven levels of development, diversity, weak Asian consciousness of the benefits of cooperation, rivalry and conflicts among big powers and political disharmony. Although the degree of Asian economic integration cannot be expected to be as high as that of Europe, even a low-level integration (for example, to establish a Pan-Asian FTA) would be a wonderful achievement. With the force of market and governments behind it Asian regional cooperation and economic integration is prospering. The boom of regional cooperation mechanisms of all sorts and scopes is a prominent feature of Asian economic integration. The coexistence of various mechanisms may continue. It is not necessary to integrate them at this early stage. It would be prudent to keep in mind that an unsuccessful mechanism might dismantle the delicate balance of Asian economic integration. When there is need for mature bilateral, trilateral and multilateral mechanisms to integrate, there would, hopefully, already be a more powerful regional integration mechanism in place which would be resistant to external impacts. Perhaps only then will Asia become a 'core' in world economic development.

References

APEC (2005). *Busan Declaration at the 13th APEC Economic Leaders' Meeting. http://www.apecsec.org.sg*

Crawford, Jo-Ann and Roberto V. Fiorentino (2005). "The Changing Landscape of Regional Trade Agreements". *http://www.wto.org*

Kumar, Nagesh (2005). "Asian Economic Community: Toward Pan-Asian Economic Integration", in *Asian Economic Cooperation and Integration*. Manila: Asian Development Bank.

Lamberte, Mario B. (2005). "An Overview of Economic Cooperation and Integration in Asia", in *Asian Economic Cooperation and Integration*. Manila: Asian Development Bank.

Linda, Law (2000). "Political Economics of RTAs under Asian Multilateral Systems". *http://www.fba.nus.edu.sg*

Lu, Jianren (2006a). "ASEAN as a Rising Power in Asia". *Global Times*, 7 February, Beijing.

———. (2006b). "Japan's Strategy on Regional Economic Cooperation", *Contemporary Asia-Pacific Studies*, No. 1, Beijing.

———. (2005). "East Asian Economic Cooperation and Its Impact to the Regional Economic Growth", *Contemporary Asia-Pacific Studies*, No. 2, Beijing.

———. (2003). "The Rise of Bilateral Free Trade Agreements in the Asia-Pacific and Its Impact to the Region", in Zhang Yunling (ed.), *Development of Regional Cooperation in the Asia-Pacific*. Beijing: World Affairs Press.

Robson, Peter (1990). *The Economics of International Integration*. London: Unuin Hyman Ltd.

Schiff, Maurice and L. Alan Winters (2002). *Regional Cooperation, and the Role of International Organisations and Regional Integration*. World Bank.

———. (2005). *Regional Integration and Development*. World Bank.

World Bank (2004). *Global Economic Prospects 2005: Trade, Regionalism and Development*.

5

Bilateral Trade and Economic Cooperation Agreements in ASEAN

Implications for Asian Economic Integration

RAHUL SEN

Introduction

The past decade witnessed a wave of 'new regionalism' engulfing the Asian economies, wherein a plethora of bilateral and regional trading and economic cooperation agreements have been mushrooming, especially in the aftermath of the regional financial crisis of 1997-98. This wave has encompassed agreements that are much more diverse in both scope and coverage than traditional Free Trade Agreements (FTAs), and are being rapidly embraced by major Asian economies as an important element of their commercial policy. Currently, almost every other economy in the Asia Pacific region is either already a signatory of or is planning to enter into such an agreement.

Indeed, Bilateral Trade and Economic Cooperation Agreements (BTAs) are increasingly being regarded by policymakers as effective and expeditious instruments for achieving trade liberalisation among 'like-minded' trading partners, as they allow governments to explore alternative paths to trade and investment liberalisation while concomitantly pursuing multilateral trade liberalisation through the WTO.

As noted by Crawford and Fiorentino (2005), the pace of new regionalism has picked up especially since the launch of the Doha Development Agenda (DDA) in November 2001, with 33 new agreements

---

Author would like to thank Mukul Asher, Sadhana Srivastava, Amarendu Nandy and Sanchita Basu Das and participants at the ICRIER Workshop on PTAs for their comments and suggestions. The usual disclaimer applies.

being notified to the WTO over the 2001-2003 period itself.[1] Most of these agreements involved Asia-Pacific economies, many of whom had hitherto been averse to bilateralism.

However, the slow progress in the Doha Round has not been the only driver behind the proliferation of FTAs in the Asia-Pacific. The post-crisis recognition by Asian policymakers that greater economic coordination and cooperation was essential to manage globalisation challenges provided an important strategic impetus for countries to enter into such agreements. Thus, FTAs in the Asia Pacific are increasingly being viewed more as a tool of foreign and economic policy than just trade policy.

With the need for an Asia-wide integration initiative gathering pace, these BTAs are indeed now being viewed as an initial step towards shaping up an Asian Economic Community in the near future. The prospects for this are being significantly debated in the wake of the first ever East Asian Summit (EAS) in Kuala Lumpur in December 2005, involving ASEAN[2]+6 countries (China, India, Japan, Korea, Australia and New Zealand). There has also been a recent proposal by Japanese Trade Minister Nikai to create a Comprehensive Economic Partnership in East Asia (CEPEA), comprising of all the 16 participants at the EAS. The argument is that an Asia-wide regional grouping would provide substantial welfare gains to all countries involved, than engaging in separate bilateral agreements, and the rest of the world would also benefit from an economically integrated Asia (Kumar, 2004, 2006; Asher and Sen, 2006).

In the above context, this paper analyses the current state of BTA proliferation in ASEAN, and its implications as a building block for a wider Pan-Asian economic community, involving ASEAN and other Asia-Pacific economies.

---

1. As of October 2003, all 146 WTO Members, with the possible exception of Mongolia, were parties to one or more of these agreements. Mongolia has recently expressed its interest to become a member of the Asia-Pacific Trade Agreement (APTA). The membership of this agreement currently includes Bangladesh, China, India, Republic of Korea, Lao People's Democratic Republic and Sri Lanka.
2. ASEAN was established on 8 August, 1967 in Bangkok by the five original Member Countries, namely, Indonesia, Malaysia, Philippines, Singapore, and Thailand. Brunei Darussalam joined on 8 January, 1984, Vietnam on 28 July, 1995, Laos and Myanmar on 23 July, 1997, and Cambodia on 30 April, 1999.

The Current State of BTAs in ASEAN

The ASEAN countries together constituted a population of about 500 million, a total area of 4.5 million square kilometres, and a combined gross domestic product of US$ 737 billion, generating a total trade of US$ 720 billion in 2004. The grouping together accounted for about 5-6 per cent share in global trade, and accounted for more than a quarter of Asia's total exports and imports during this period. Since its inception, ASEAN economies have traditionally been outward-looking and have been significantly dependent on trade and foreign direct investment (FDI) flows for their growth prospects.

Initially, the emphasis of ASEAN members was on enhancing peace and promoting stability in the region. It was only in 1992 that serious efforts were launched towards increasing intra-ASEAN trade through the Framework Agreement on Enhancing Economic Cooperation which was adopted at the fourth ASEAN Summit in Singapore that included the launching of the ASEAN Free Trade Area or the AFTA.

Until the year 2001, AFTA was the only FTA involving the 10-member ASEAN economies. This agreement was restricted only to trade in goods and involved a phased elimination of tariffs on intra-ASEAN trade. The AFTA is now by and large fully implemented for the older ASEAN members, namely, Brunei, Indonesia, Malaysia, Philippines, Singapore and Thailand, with the newer members expected to comply with it by the year 2010. However, it is important to note that, for certain specific categories of products, a few of the older ASEAN members have not yet fully complied with AFTA guidelines. It is also important to note that this agreement involved only a 40 per cent value-added (VA) cumulative rules of origin (RoO) for non-originating goods—one of the simplest RoO to be administered under any FTA.

However, with the economic and financial crisis of 1997-98 adversely impacting the growth prospects of ASEAN countries, and a concomitant impasse at the WTO meeting at Seattle in 1999, highly trade-dependent countries in ASEAN—for example, Singapore—began to embark on bilateralism to enhance the free trade agenda. Thus, the current wave of FTAs in ASEAN was initiated by the signing of a first bilateral FTA in ASEAN involving Singapore and New Zealand in 2001, termed as the Agreement between New Zealand and Singapore for a Closer Economic Partnership (ANZSCEP). Notably, this agreement had no exclusion of products from its tariff elimination list and was very comprehensive covering liberalisation and facilitation of trade in services, investments, trade facilitation, government procurement and intellectual property protection. This signalled the intention to enter into WTO-plus FTAs that were consistent with the WTO, and also provide avenues to negotiate complex issues bilaterally on which consensus has not yet been reached multilaterally.

Taking serious note of this shift of Singapore towards bilateralism, several other ASEAN countries, for example, Thailand, and more recently Malaysia and Philippines, have subsequently jumped onto the bilateral FTA bandwagon, negotiating several agreements that are still in the pipeline. As noted by Sally and Sen (2005), trade policy in Southeast Asia is now dominated by BTAs, with a domino effect being observed in other Asian countries, namely, India, China, Japan and Korea. These countries had hitherto been strong advocates of multilateralism but are now creating their own BTA hubs around them.[3]

With BTA proliferation in Asia being a dynamic activity, new initiatives are being announced frequently, and it is increasingly becoming difficult to determine an exact figure on the number of existing and proposed BTAs involving ASEAN (and its individual members). While Angtkeiwicz and Whalley (2005) estimate that within 2005, about seven such agreements have proliferated among ASEAN countries as a regional grouping, this number is a conservative estimate as it does not include the individual bilateral initiatives being negotiated or proposed by the ASEAN member countries.

Table 5.1 provides details on the progress of all the BTAs in ASEAN that are being proposed or are being negotiated by these countries. The following trends seem to emerge:

- First, there is the emergence of an overall pattern of ASEAN forging greater economic linkages with Asia-Pacific through its BTAs with China, India, Japan, Korea, Australia and New

3. See Sen (2005) and Plummer (2006) for analysis of BTA proliferation in Asia.

Table 5.1

Summary of BTA Proliferation in ASEAN: 2001-Till Date

Country/ Groupings	*Partner Country*	*Combined Market Size, 2004 (No. of consumers, millions)*	*Rules of Origin (RoO)*	*Areas of Coverage*	*Expected Date of Implementation*
ASEAN	China	1841	Based on the ASEAN CEPT rules using the value-added approach with a 40 per cent local content; include product specific rules	Framework Agreement for FTA: Establishment of within 10 years: FTA for Trade in Goods to be realised by 2010 for ASEAN-6 and 2015 for the new members; FTA for Trade in Services and Investment; Early Harvest Programme; Cooperation in other areas of mutual interest	EHP implemented on 1 Jan, 04; intend to conclude the agreement by 2010
	India	1624	Negotiations ongoing	Framework Agreement for RTIA: Parties agree to negotiate in order to establish a RTIA, which includes a FTA in goods, services and investment, and broader economic cooperation	Initial commitments on tariff reduction to begin on 1 Jan, 07; committed to reduce and eliminate tariffs by 2011 for ASEAN-6 and by 2016 for LDCs
	Japan	672	Cumulative rules of origin	Framework agreement for CEP: Liberalisation of trade in goods, services and investment by 2012; facilitation and promotion of trade and investment; economic and technical cooperation in energy, ICT, SME	Negotiations on-going; committed to conclude by mid-2007

Contd...

...contd...

Country/ Groupings	*Partner Country*	*Combined Market Size, 2004 (No. of consumers, millions)*	*Rules of Origin (RoO)*	*Areas of Coverage*	*Expected Date of Implementation*
	Korea	593	Negotiations on RoO ongoing and expected to conclude by Ma 06	FTA for Trade in Goods to be realised by 2012 for ASEAN-6, 2018 for Vietnam and 2020 for Cambodia, Lao PDR and Myanmar; FTA for Trade in Services and Investment	FTA in goods is expected to enter into force in mid-2006
	CER (Australia and New Zealand)	569	Negotiation ongoing	Framework agreement for CEP: Comprehensive covering trade in goods, services and investment, goal is to double trade and investment between the region by 2010; negotiation for FTA started in 2005	Fifth meeting scheduled for April 2006
Indonesia	Japan	345	TBN	Under negotiations	TBN
Malaysia	Japan	153	Product specific rules	Both FTA component and bilateral economic cooperation; tariff concessions over 10 years with flexibility for selected sensitive products; covers: trade in goods and services, investment, intellectual property, enhancement of business environment	Negotiations concluded in Oct. 05 and Agreement was signed on 13 Dec., 05
	USA	319	Negotiation ongoing	Covers trade and investment, protection of intellectual property, small and medium size enterprises, ICT, MRAs	Joint Council Meetings are in progress

...contd...

...contd...

Country/ Groupings	*Partner Country*	*Combined Market Size, 2004 (No. of consumers, millions)*	*Rules of Origin (RoO)*	*Areas of Coverage*	*Expected Date of Implementation*
	Australia	45	Negotiation ongoing	Bilateral FTA covers both trade and investment; address both tariff and non-tariff measures; MRAs to facilitate trade	Conclude by mid-2006; Third meeting scheduled in March 2006
	NZ	29	Negotiation ongoing	Covers both trade in goods and services; address both tariff and non-tariff measures; promote investment	Sixth meeting scheduled in mid-April 2006
	Chile	41	TBN	JSG will submit its recommendations by the end of 2006	JSG established in Jan. 06
	Korea	73	Negotiation ongoing	FTA covers—trade in goods and services; investment promotion and facilitation; and economic and technical cooperation	Negotiations going in line with ASEAN-Korea FTA
	India	1105	TBN	Full FTA: Trade in goods and services, and investments; Comprehensive services and FDI covered; economic cooperation activities in areas of mutual interest	Draft Joint Study Report is finalised
	Pakistan	177	TBN	Covers—trade in goods and services, and investments; incorporate an early harvest programme; economic cooperation activities in areas of mutual interest	EHP implemented on 1 Jan, 2006; expected to implement the full-FTA by early 2007

...contd...

...contd...

Country/ Groupings	*Partner Country*	*Combined Market Size, 2004 (No. of consumers, millions)*	*Rules of Origin (RoO)*	*Areas of Coverage*	*Expected Date of Implementation*
Philippines	Japan	211	Negotiation ongoing	Covers trade in goods, easing restrictions in Japan's labour market to accommodate more Filipino healthcare professionals; lowering tariffs on agricultural trade; liberalising investment conditions; coordination in science and technology, energy and SMEs	Agreement expected to complete in 2006, currently stalled as legally challenged
	USA	376	TBN	TBN	Proposed but no negotiations as yet
Singapore	Australia	24	General RoO: 30 per cent or 50 per cent local value content	Full FTA: Comprehensive; negative list in services, FDI covered; separate, additional commitments for financial services to transparent market access; measures on movement of person included; builds on TRIPS; Government Procurement covered	In force from July 2003
	Canada	36	Negotiation ongoing	Covers trade in goods and services, financial services, investment, government procurement, institutional provisions and dispute settlement.	Under negotiations
	Egypt	73	Negotiation ongoing	Full FTA: Negotiations started in 2004	Under negotiations

...contd...

...contd...

Country/ Groupings	*Partner Country*	*Combined Market Size, 2004 (No. of consumers, millions)*	*Rules of Origin (RoO)*	*Areas of Coverage*	*Expected Date of Implementation*
	EFTA	17	Complicated product specific	Full FTA: Comprehensive; FDI fully covered, IPP included, refers to WTO Government Procurement Agreement	2000
	India	1084	General 40 per cent rule; but includes product specific rules as well	Full FTA: Comprehensive services and FDI broadly covered; negative list in services; measures on movement of persons included; commitment to develop IPR cooperation	2005
	Japan	132	Product specific rules	Full FTA: Comprehensive; negative list in services; separate financial-services and capital market development measures; FDI fully covered; IPR included	2002
	Jordan	10	Complicated product specific RoO	Full FTA: Comprehensive; separate provision for textiles, investment governed by separate bilateral treaty; IPR refers to WTO commitments	2004
	Korea	52	Complicated RoO; product specific rules that apply only to non-originating materials	Full FTA: Comprehensive; 10 year implementation; negative list in services; FDI and financial services is broadly included; some sector specific commitments for financial services; provisions on movement of persons; builds on TRIPS	Implemented from March 2006

contd

...contd...

Country/ Groupings	*Partner Country*	*Combined Market Size, 2004 (No. of consumers, millions)*	*Rules of Origin (RoO)*	*Areas of Coverage*	*Expected Date of Implementation*
	Mexico	108		Signed a Joint Declaration on the Mexico-Singapore FTA in 2000	
	NZ	8	General VA rule (40 Per cent)	Full FTA: Comprehensive; negative list in services; FDI fully covered; IPR included	January 2001
	Sri Lanka	24	TBN	Comprehensive Economic Partnership Agreement: FTA for the liberalisation of trade in goods and services, investment liberalisation and other cooperation elements	Under negotiation
	USA	298	Complicated product specific RoO, including "Integrated Sourcing Initiative"	Full FTA: Highly comprehensive; 10 yr. implementation; restrictive mainly in textiles; negative list in services; capital control only as safeguard, FDI covered; extends WTO TRIPS; builds on WTO government Procurement	Jan 2004
	Qatar	5	Negotiation ongoing	Comprehensive agreement; covers trade in goods, services (including financial services), e-commerce, investment, government procurement, customs, and media cooperation	Finalising the text of the agreement, is expected to be completed shortly

...contd...

...contd...

Country/ Groupings	*Partner Country*	*Combined Market Size, 2004 (No. of consumers, millions)*	*Rules of Origin (RoO)*	*Areas of Coverage*	*Expected date of implementation*
	Peru	32	Negotiation ongoing	Announced FTA on Nov 19, 2004; Negotiations are targeted to commence in 2006: liberalise trade in goods, services and investments	Expected to be completed by 2007.
	Panama	7	A product qualifies if at least 35 per cent value addition has taken place, or if the product satisfies a product-specific rule	comprehensive agreement, covers trade in goods and services, customs procedures, financial services, investment, telecommunications, e-commerce, competition policy and government procurement	Concluded on March 1, 2006
	Kuwait	7	Negotiation ongoing	FTA covers trade in goods, customs, investment, and government procurement. Discussions continuing on services, financial services and other legal aspects	Under negotiation
	Bahrain	5	Negotiation ongoing	TBN, expected to be comprehensive	Finished preliminary discussion
	Brunei, NZ, Chile	25	Completed and product specific RoO	Full FTA: Not fully comprehensive; Negative list in services that excludes financial services; FDI not covered; builds on TRIPS; Government Procurement extensively covered	2005

...contd...

...contd...

Country/ Groupings	*Partner Country*	*Combined Market Size, 2004 (No. of consumers, millions)*	*Rules of Origin (RoO)*	*Areas of Coverage*	*Expected Date of Implementation*
	UAE	9	TBN	Under study	TBN
	South Africa	50	TBN	TBN	Proposed, TBN
Brunei	Singapore, NZ, Chile	25	Completed and product specific RoO	Full FTA: Not fully comprehensive; Negative list in services that's excludes financial services; FDI not covered; builds on TRIPS; Government Procurement extensively covered	2005
Thailand	Australia	83	Complicated, product specific	Full FTA: Comprehensive; special safeguard measures for sensitive agricultural goods; services broadly included and FDI fully covered; builds on TRIPS	2005
	Bahrain	63	40 per cent VA rule	Trade in goods, safeguards	
	China	1359	Direct consignment requirement	"Early Harvest" on agricultural produce	In force from 2003
	India	1142	Interim RoO applied	Early Harvest Scheme: Allow concessional tariffs on 82 items (mainly electronic and auto components)	Signed a Framework agreement in 2004; trade in goods agreement reached
	Japan	190	TBN	Economic Partnership Agreement; FTA negotiations cover issues — trade in goods and services, investment, intellectual property rights, agriculture, competition policy	Postponed the signing of EPA till the Thai political picture is more clear

...contd...

...contd...

Country/ Groupings	*Partner Country*	*Combined Market Size, 2004 (No. of consumers, millions)*	*Rules of Origin (RoO)*	*Areas of Coverage*	*Expected Date of Implementation*
	Korea	111	TBN	TBN	Proposed
	NZ	66	Complicated, product specific	FTA covers liberalisation of trade in goods; addressed tariff elimination; agreement on trade in services would be covered within three years.	FTA came into effect in July 2005.
	Peru	90	TBN	TBN	Negotiations ongoing; eliminate tariffs on trade in goods by 2015
	South Africa	108	TBN	TBN	Proposed
	USA	356	TBN	FTA covers investment, services, government procurement, intellectual property, and agriculture	Last round of talks held in January 2006; suspended further talks until the new government comes.
	BIMSTEC	1439	TBN	Trade in goods, services, investment, trade facilitation	Agreement on trade in goods to be negotiated by 2006
	EFTA	75	TBN	TBN	TBN

Notes: N.B: Although Lao, Myanmar, and Cambodia are excluded from this Table, it is important to note that Laos is a signatory to the APTA agreement, while Myanmar is a part of the Bay of Bengal Initiative for Multi-sectoral and Technical Economic Cooperation (BIMSTEC), which signed a framework agreement towards creating an FTA in 2006.

TBN: To be negotiated.

Bay of Bengal Initiative for Muti-Sectoral Technical and Economic Cooperation (BIMSTEC) members: Bangladesh, India, Myanmar, Sri Lanka, Thailand, Nepal and Bhutan.

European Free Trade Association (EFTA) members: Switzerland, Liechtenstein, Norway, Iceland.

Source: Compiled by author from various government and news sources.

Zealand.[4] Although most of the ASEAN initiatives have involved partner countries from Asia, BTAs of Singapore and, in particular, Thailand, have also involved negotiations with trading partners from other parts of the world, including North America, Latin America and the African countries. In this context, it is important to note that Singapore has entered for the first time into a plurilateral and cross-regional Trans-Pacific Strategic Economic Partnership (SEP) agreement involving Brunei from ASEAN as well and New Zealand and Chile, which involves a combined market of about 25 million consumers. In contrast, the potential BTA in ASEAN which constitutes the biggest market size is that of the ASEAN-China FTA, with a combined market of 1.8 billion consumers, followed by an ASEAN-India FTA (1.6 billion consumers).

- Second, among all the BTA initiatives launched so far in ASEAN since 2001, the ones that have been mostly implemented and are currently in force are Singapore's BTAs (involving New Zealand, Japan, EFTA, Australia, the United States, Jordan, India and Korea) and Thailand's BTAs (involving Bahrain, Australia and New Zealand).[5] Apart from these, most of the other initiatives are either at the stage of being studied before formal negotiations, or are in the process of negotiation. Thus, the likely content and coverage of many of these agreements and their possible impacts on regional and global trading patterns remain yet unknown.
- Third, the BTA activity in ASEAN ranges from that of limited BTAs on trade in goods with large exclusion lists and limited product coverage to that of highly comprehensive bilateral agreements. This is especially so of the BTAs involving Singapore, that cover not just trade in goods, but also services, investments, non-tariff barriers and regulatory measures for trade and investments. Moreover, they also include complex issues of

4. ASEAN is contemplating to enter into BTA negotiations with the US, the EU, Pakistan and Russia in 2006.

5. Thailand has entered into a framework agreement for a BTA with India in 2004, which currently involves tariff elimination only on 82 selected goods. Although the framework agreement indicates this FTA will be comprehensive, there has not been significant progress after the Early Harvest Scheme.

government procurement, competition policy and intellectual property protection that have not yet been put on the agenda for negotiations at the multilateral level under the auspices of the WTO. It is significant to note that most of the other BTAs of ASEAN have not included these issues in the negotiations so far, or have very broad provisions that do not include much substance.[6]

- Fourth, a variety of rules of origin to determine preferential treatment for non-originating goods has been applied or is currently being negotiated across ASEAN BTAs. It is observed that while the VA rule is generally applied across Singapore's BTAs, a mix of other criteria, such as the change in tariff classification (CTC) and other restrictive rules, have also been applied. Even in other ASEAN FTAs, restrictive rules seem to have prevailed over simple ones.
- Fifth, there is a great deal of overlapping among the BTA partners of ASEAN and the individual member countries. Thus, while Singapore has already implemented its agreements with New Zealand, Australia, India, Korea and Japan, it is also a negotiating member in ASEAN-wide BTA initiatives with these countries. Similarly, Malaysia and Thailand, that are negotiating a bilateral agreement with Japan, India, Australia, New Zealand and Korea, are also involved as part of the ASEAN-wide negotiations with these same set of countries.

Many, from among this diverse range of BTA initiatives in ASEAN, also do not seem to be driven by economic rationale. This becomes evident from the fact that the United States and the European Union (EU) are among the most important trading partners for ASEAN members (Table 5.2), but till date, there have been no negotiations that are ongoing among ASEAN and the EU and the United States. The United States only has one enforced BTA with Singapore, and is currently negotiating with Thailand and Malaysia, without much significant progress. The EU is currently contemplating to negotiate an ASEAN-wide BTA in the near future.

6. See Banda and Whalley (2005) for a detailed analysis of non-trade issues dealt in the ASEAN-FTAs.

Table 5.2

Trade Shares of ASEAN's Bilateral Trade with Its Current and Proposed BTA Partners, 2004

Country/ Grouping	*Partners*	*Share in Total Trade, 2004 (Per cent)*	*Share in Exports, 2004 (Per cent)*	*Share in Imports, 2004 (Per cent)*
ASEAN-6	China	8.5	7.6	9.4
	India	1.9	2.3	1.5
	Japan	12.2	10.4	14.0
	Korea	4.4	4.0	4.8
	USA	14.4	15.4	13.4
	CER	2.95	3.6	2.3
	EU	12.65	13.4	11.9
Vietnam*	USA	12.1	19.6	4.5
	Japan	13.1	14.4	11.8
	Sri Lanka	0.04	0.03	0.04
	Korea	6.4	2.4	10.4
Brunei*	Singapore	12.3	4.50	20.10
	New Zealand	1.3	2.30	0.20
	Chile^	0.01	NA	0.01
Thailand*	Australia	2.4	2.7	2.1
	Bahrain	0.1	0.1	0.1
	China	7.6	7.1	8.0
	India	1.0	0.8	1.2
	Japan	19.2	14.2	24.1
	Korea	2.9	2.0	3.8
	New Zealand	0.3	0.3	0.3
	Peru	0.0	0.0	0.1
	South Africa	0.5	0.5	0.4
	USA	13.3	17.0	9.5
	BIMSTEC	2.2	1.9	2.4
	EFTA	1.2	1.2	1.1

Contd...

...contd...

Country/ Grouping	*Partners*	*Share in Total Trade, 2004 (Per cent)*	*Share in Exports, 2004 (Per cent)*	*Share in Imports, 2004 (Per cent)*
Malaysia	Japan	13.1	10.1	16.1
	USA	16.7	18.8	14.6
	Australia	2.5	3.3	1.7
	New Zealand	0.4	0.4	0.3
	EU	11.9	11.8	11.9
	Korea	4.3	3.5	5
	India	1.8	2.4	1.2
	Pakistan	0.3	0.6	0.05
Philippines	Japan	18.8	20.1	17.4
	USA	18.5	18.2	18.8
Singapore	Australia	2.6	3.7	1.4
	Canada	0.4	0.3	0.4
	Egypt	0.1	0.07	0.2
	EFTA#	1.0	0.4	1.6
	EU	13.3	13.7	12.8
	India	2.0	2.3	1.7
	Japan	9.1	6.5	11.7
	Jordan	0.02	0.02	0.01
	Korea	4.2	4.1	4.3
	Mexico	0.4	0.5	0.3
	New Zealand	0.4	0.5	0.2
	Sri Lanka	0.2	0.3	0.04
	USA	12.8	13	12.6
	Qatar	0.6	0.05	1.2
	Peru	0.01	0.01	0.01
	Panama	0.4	0.7	0.01
	Kuwait	1.0	0.04	1.9
	Bahrain	0.0	0.02	0.05
	Brunei	0.2	0.3	0.09
	Chile	0.03	0.01	0.05

Notes: * indicates 2003 figures.

Source: Computed from UN Comtrade Database.

It is also observed that for ASEAN, Japan is the largest BTA partner in Asia, constituting 12.2 per cent of ASEAN's total merchandise trade, followed by China (9.4 per cent), Korea (4.8 per cent) and India (1.5 per cent). ASEAN is expected to enforce its BTAs with all these countries and with CER (Australia-New Zealand) by the year 2015.

However, Table 5.2 also indicates that ASEAN's bilateral trade shares with a number of their non-Asian BTA partners is insignificant, not even accounting for 1-2 per cent of total merchandise trade of individual ASEAN members. This indicates that gains from merchandise trade for ASEAN through a BTA with these countries are likely to be minimal. This is particularly so in the case of Singapore and Thailand's BTAs with Latin America and Middle Eastern countries. Presumably, the rationale behind entering into these BTAs is to explore gains from economic cooperation in other areas, that is, services, investments and broader economic cooperation initiatives, whose importance in the trading relationship cannot be suitably quantified.

The above analysis indicates that BTA activity in ASEAN has been prolific over the 2001-2006 period, and promises to increasingly gather pace in the future. Recognising this reality of BTA proliferation in ASEAN, Indonesia, the largest ASEAN member and the only one to resist entering into BTAs so far, has already begun its first BTA negotiations with Japan and discussions are ongoing for a similar bilateral deal with India. This is an important indication of the domino effect that other BTAs of ASEAN are having on Indonesia.

It is estimated by Sen (2005) that if the proposed and currently negotiated BTAs do come into force and their preferences are effectively utilised, nearly half or more of ASEAN and India's merchandise trade is going to be driven by 'new regionalism', while such BTAs would cover about a quarter or more of China's total merchandise trade. Given the increasing proliferation of new agreements, even this could indeed be a conservative estimate. The above figures confirm the fact that BTAs are now the reality in ASEAN and elsewhere in Asia, and are likely to be so in the foreseeable future, especially if a satisfactory outcome is not forthcoming through the multilateral process. This possibility is beginning to look increasingly likely, with most of the WTO members busy negotiating BTAs, devoting less of their scarce negotiating resources to multilateral negotiations.

Perceived Benefits from ASEAN BTAs:[7] The Policymakers' View

Why is ASEAN going towards the BTA route? The general view among many policymakers in ASEAN, and increasingly in the rest of Asia, is that there are several perceived benefits from entering into BTAs, apart from that of gaining greater market access, and lowering business costs by reduction of tariff barriers. First, it is being increasingly believed that BTAs that involve economic partnership agreements, which are comprehensive and involve deeper liberalisation beyond tariff reduction in goods, can provide a catalyst for enhancing the pace of multilateral trade liberalisation. This is through a domino effect on non-members, who would want to avoid being discriminated and, therefore, forced to liberalise faster, as is now evident in the Indonesian context. Further, FTAs serve as a 'testing ground' for negotiating complex issues bilaterally, and can set a precedent for negotiating them multilaterally among a larger group of countries.

Second, it is also believed that legal provisions of the BTAs can lock-in policy reforms, particularly in the areas of the services sector and investment liberalisation which are otherwise difficult to undertake at the multilateral level. BTAs can be used by governments to facilitate reforms in their economy, thus improving their competitiveness. However, it is important to note that, barring Singapore's BTAs, most of the other ASEAN BTAs have not yet negotiated services and investment liberalisation, and thus have not initiated any domestic reforms measures through these BTAs.

The third, and perhaps one of the most important perceived benefits from BTAs, is the ability to provide a positive signal towards enhancing economic and strategic cooperation, and addressing regional security concerns.[8] Majority of the recent BTAs, which are in the form of

---

7. This section draws on Sen (2005).

8. This was one of the motives behind India negotiating a Comprehensive Economic Cooperation Agreement (CECA) with Singapore, which provided a strong signal for the desire of India to forge economic and strategic links with ASEAN and East Asian countries.

broader economic partnership agreements, facilitate members to enhance their economic as well as strategic links, since both the members become important stakeholders in liberalising and facilitating trade, investment and economic cooperation and are, therefore, committed to maintaining peace and stability between them. Inclusion of economic and technical cooperation in areas such as energy, IT and industrial cooperation embody the strategic element of these BTAs. This, particularly, is an important motive for those ASEAN countries that need to address regional security concerns. Liang (2005), a Singapore policymaker, notes:

> Beyond advancing its economic interests, Singapore believes that these intra and inter-regional FTAs help to build a web of strategic linkages for Singapore within the region and with countries outside the region. They serve the broader strategic interest of anchoring the presence of its major trading partners in South East Asia, and ensuring that they remain stakeholders in Singapore and the region. This web of interlocking economic and strategic interests helps contribute to regional stability, security and prosperity.

The above reason perhaps explains why ASEAN members like Singapore and Thailand are seeking BTAs with Middle Eastern and Latin American countries whose economic links with them, as observed in Table 5.2, are, at best, minimal.

Concerns from ASEAN FTAs: From Spaghetti to Noodle Bowl?

The above analysis notwithstanding, it has been traditionally argued in the literature on preferential trading and its welfare implications for developing countries[9] that bilateral route to trade liberalisation is a Pareto-inferior option, and is unlikely to be welfare enhancing since it may lead to trade diversion wherein, when a BTA shifts import sources from a more efficient supplier (low-cost) to a less efficient (higher cost) supplier in a member country, that causes reduction in national welfare. In the current context, wherein investment is also being negotiated through BTAs, there is an additional possibility of investment diversion as well. However, as observed by Banda and Whalley (2005), the current complexity of BTAs beyond goods and

9. Bhagwati (1993), Baldwin (1993), Bhagwati and Panagariya (1996), Winters (1998).

services have negated the possibility of applying modelling techniques of modern trade theory to evaluate the precise impact of these BTAs on economic welfare.

Figure 5.1

BTA Network in the Asia-Pacific as of 2006

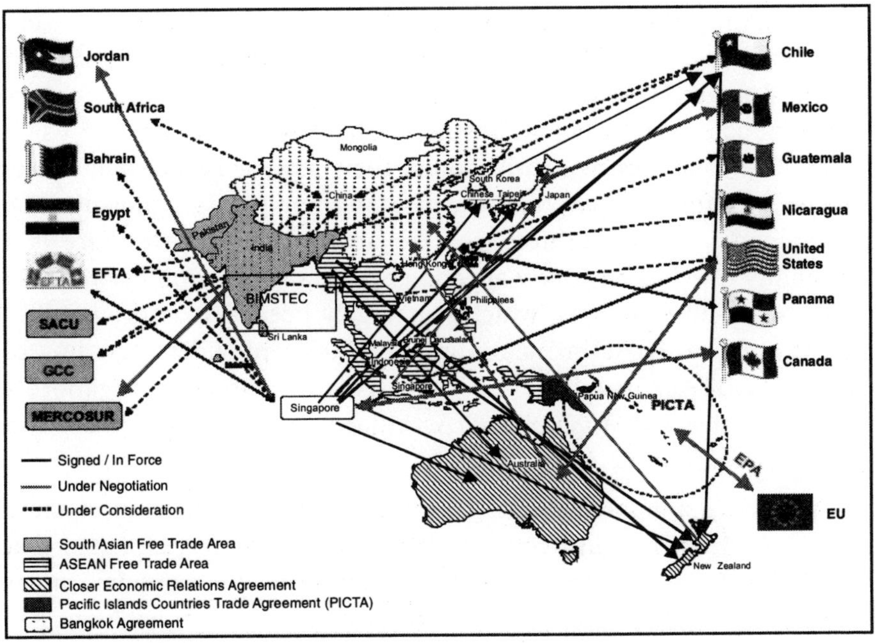

Source: Adapted from Crawford and Fiorentino (2005).

The concerns from the proliferation of ASEAN BTAs are manifold. First, at the outset, these BTAs create a complex hubs and spokes network of overlapping BTAs within Asia, with a potential for trade diversion away from the spokes towards the emerging hub of these BTAs. As observed in Figure 5.1, there is no single hub for ASEAN BTAs, what with ASEAN as a group, as well as Singapore, Thailand and, increasingly, others, creating multiple BTA hubs. At the same time, India, China and Korea are also creating their own BTA hubs. The result is a multitude of BTA hubs wherein a spoke country in one BTA is becoming a hub in another. This situation, referred to as a 'noodle bowl' of BTAs in the Asian context,[10] reduces the overall

10. Baldwin (2006).

welfare impact, especially as each of the countries involved is entering into a bilateral deal with the same trading partner.

As observed in Table 5.1, the second concern stems from the application of a variety of (RoOs) with respect to preferential trade liberalisation in goods in this hub and spoke network of BTAs. These rules of origin are complex and costly for businesses to comply with, thus negating the very purpose of a BTA to reduce business costs. Referred to as the 'spaghetti bowl' argument in Bhagwati (1995) and also in Krueger (1997), this is manifesting itself as a far more complex Asian 'noodle bowl' wherein businesses have to either consider using these BTAs and, consequently, adjust their strategies for compliance, or else continue to pay MFN tariffs for their goods, ignoring BTA preferences. If these preferences are utilised in ASEAN there is a possibility of BTAs adversely affecting existing production networks in ASEAN and in East Asia, which has largely been market-driven. In a recent study of BTAs in Asia Plummer (2006) provides a grading of ASEAN's BTAs, in which he indicates that even in Singapore's comprehensive and WTO-plus BTAs, rules of origin are restrictive and limit scope for trade expansion.

The above argument relates to the question of utilisation of these BTAs, which is the third concern. It has been recently estimated that AFTA, ASEAN's first regional trade liberalisation agreement, which has one of the simplest rules of origin for tariff preferences, has remained grossly underutilised at about 5 per cent of total trade, with many exporters preferring to pay the MFN tariffs instead. With new BTAs being proliferated and each BTA being different, and requiring different conditions for compliance, businesses have to devise new strategies to utilise BTAs. They not only need to understand the rules of origin and match its requirement for each FTA partner if exporting to multiple countries, but also need to understand the entry requirements as a service provider and the conditions to be fulfilled for granting temporary entry. These involve significant adjustment costs. It is, therefore, no surprise that negotiations in current ASEAN BTAs have generated minimal business interest, raising concerns as to whether preferences under ASEAN BTAs would indeed be utilised. There is, therefore, an urgent need to involve more business participation in BTA negotiations to ensure that they are utilised upon completion.

Fourth, the proliferation of new regionalism through BTAs is likely to lead to inefficient utilisation of scarce negotiating resources that could be otherwise devoted towards multilateral negotiations in the WTO. This has particularly serious implications for negotiators of those low and middle-income developing countries in ASEAN that are small in number, lack technocratic and institutional capacity to negotiate bilateral BTAs and are sometimes forced to end up making too many compromises in a BTA that could have adverse welfare implications for their economies in the long run.

Fifth, with individual ASEAN members having already enforced some of their own bilateral deals with major trading partners, the issue that remains to be resolved is how these countries are to treat the ASEAN-wide agreements with the same trading partners, once they are enforced. It is yet not clear whether regional agreements would subsume these bilateral deals, thus posing a concern as to their applicability and consistency in the negotiating framework.[11] However, with no common framework for negotiations evolving so far in ASEAN, the possibility of bilateral deals being subsumed by regional ones seems remote.

Finally, it is important to note that apart from differences in terms of the rules of origin, there also exist dissimilarities in these BTAs with respect to the choice of their major internal parameters (the depth of trade liberalisation commitments and sectoral coverage) that constitute the negotiating framework.[12] These create serious concerns that such BTAs are emerging more as stumbling blocks rather than the building blocks of global free trade. There is a possibility that the perceived benefits from greater liberalisation and stronger strategic links may override these concerns. The net economic impact of these BTAs remains to be seen.

Implications for Asian Economic Integration

The idea of an Asian Economic Community stems from the fact that unlike North America and Europe, which enforced two regional trading agreements through the North American Free Trade Agreement

---

11. Rajan and Sen (2005).

12. Sen (2005) study of ASEAN, China and India's BTAs for further details.

(NAFTA) and the EU in the 1990s, there have been no Pan-Asian efforts towards regionalism. The need for this was recognised more acutely by Asian policymakers in the wake of the financial and economic crisis of 1997-98, which demonstrated the need for greater economic cooperation and coordination to better manage globalisation challenges.

It is in the above context that Kumar (2004, 2006) supports the formation of JACIK as an initial start to developing a Pan-Asian economic community. He observes that JACIK economies together constitute a market that is growing more rapidly than that of the rest of the world, is likely to be equivalent to that of the EU in terms of GDP, its total merchandise trade higher than that of NAFTA members, and its international reserves more than those of the EU and NAFTA combined. It is, therefore, argued that a pan-Asian economic integration can exploit the complementarities among the Asian economies to create synergies for mutual benefit. Kumar (2006) specifically notes:

> Substantial complementarities exist between Asian economies that remain to be exploited for their mutual common benefit. For instance, while the region has economies that are surplus in capital resources, there are also economies, which have inadequate domestic savings for rapid development. The region is similarly characterised by complementarities in the demand and supply of other resources such as technology, and skilled manpower.

As noted by Asher and Srivastava (2003), India's role in this process of formation of the JACIK or a similar Asia-wide economic grouping is likely to be crucial, given its significant complementarities with East Asian economies, in the areas of trade, investments, science and technology, energy security and skilled manpower availability, among others. They note that India's ongoing calibrated globalisation, and its gradual integration with the world economy in a market-consistent manner have created a favourable environment for its role in deepening economic linkages with East Asia. This has already been recognised through India's participation in the Second EAS in January 2007, wherein it was a signatory to the Cebu Declaration on East Asian Energy Security for improving energy efficiency and reducing dependence on fossil fuels, along with 15 other EAS members in Asia.

By developing a network of BTAs within Asia, ASEAN has already, in some sense, laid the foundation towards an Asian economic integration. However, it is important to note that regionalism in ASEAN is operating both at the bilateral and regional levels. While ASEAN recognises the importance of engaging the rest of Asia through BTAs, it is also increasingly conscious of the fact that economic integration will help it to maximise the complementarities among member countries to achieve economies of scale, and become an efficient manufacturer of products, especially in the wake of the economic rise of China. Deeper economic integration among ASEAN, while improving its competitiveness, will place it in a better position to gain as a BTA hub.

It is in the above context that ASEAN has embarked upon creating an ASEAN Economic Community by the year 2020, as envisaged by the Bali Concord II in 2003. This envisages ASEAN developing into a common market with free trade in goods and services and free movement of capital and labour by the year 2020. This is indeed an ambitious agenda, involving well-developed institutional and legal infrastructure to facilitate economic integration. Given that most of the ASEAN countries have only implemented AFTA, with not much progress of regional liberalisation of services and investments, implementing the concept of the Asian Economic Community (AEC) remains challenging. Although a high-level task force has been constituted to implement the process of economic integration and 11 priority sectors identified for fast-track integration, the rate of progress appears to be rather slow, as observed by Hew and Sen (2004). They also indicate that the AEC needs a clear and comprehensive blueprint with action plans, deadlines and milestones to be achieved, and that sacrificing sovereignty for deeper economic integration may be difficult for some ASEAN governments.

Nevertheless, the seriousness of ASEAN policymakers in preparing for the AEC seems to be evident from the fact that an eminent persons' group has been constituted to frame an ASEAN Charter, which will provide the necessary legal entity to ASEAN to institutionalise economic integration (Severino 2005). This charter is expected to take shape in the upcoming ASEAN Summit in Singapore in 2007.

On the other hand, ASEAN is concomitantly entering into Economic Partnership Agreements (EPAs) with a number of its trading partners. These agreements, if utilised effectively, have the potential to be the building blocks of a future AEC, with an economically integrated ASEAN as its core. However, in its present state, most ASEAN BTAs are largely unconnected from each other, with Singapore having already implemented a number of its comprehensive BTAs with the major players in Asian economic integration—Japan, India and Korea—and negotiating as a partner in the ASEAN-China FTA. As Plummer (2006) observes, most of Singapore's BTAs are of the 'building block' type and are generally WTO-plus in nature, except where restrictions of rules of origin exist. He observes that ASEAN BTAs that have involved developed-country partners are fairly liberal in content and coverage, except for the rules of origin.

Notably, apart from Singapore, none of the ASEAN members have yet strived to implement such comprehensive BTAs. Most of them are at the negotiating stage, and in some cases only an 'Early Harvest Scheme' for tariff elimination on a few select goods has been agreed upon. This implies that while Singapore might be in a position to utilise BTAs as a building block for Asian economic integration, other ASEAN members are not quite in a position to do so at the moment, mainly due to being at a different level of economic development than the city-state. Unlike Singapore, most of the ASEAN members have a sizeable domestic sector, with the agriculture sector making an important contribution to those economies. This leads to political sensitivities complicating the negotiations process.

It is also important to note that in the pursuit of quickly negotiating BTAs, many developing ASEAN members are ignoring unilateral liberalisation and are not pursuing important domestic economic reforms which are critical for their growth prospects and to sustain competitiveness. As observed by Sally and Sen (2005), the engine of liberalisation and regulatory reform by ASEAN countries has to be home driven, with BTAs playing a supportive role. Lessons from China and India are important for ASEAN in this regard, since both countries are pursuing unilateral liberalisation, apart from bilateral and multilateral tracks of trade policy, and have significantly improved their growth prospects.

The above literature implies that ASEAN has to strengthen its efforts towards regionalism both at the bilateral and regional levels in order to play a more effective role in fostering Asian economic integration.

Conclusion

While East Asian economic integration has been largely market driven, BTAs have now become a reality, with ASEAN and its individual members creating a network of BTAs around the major economies of Asia. While they are largely targeted as strategic instruments for achieving closer economic cooperation in Asia, they have the potential to be the building blocks towards deeper economic integration. However, in its present state, there are valid concerns that, if not effectively implemented and not properly designed, these BTAs could instead end up being the stumbling blocks towards this effort.

The paper has indicated that, in their present state, BTAs in Asia constitute a wide mix, with Singapore's full comprehensive BTAs on one hand, and limited agreements on trade in goods by most ASEAN members, on the other. At the same time, ASEAN is also striving towards deeper regional economic integration, in order to improve its competitiveness and gain from being a BTA hub with other Asian economies. These two processes need to reinforce each other in order for ASEAN to foster deeper economic integration in Asia.

It may be concluded from the above analysis that not only does ASEAN require to develop institutional and legal infrastructure for economic integration, it also needs to ensure that the welfare gains from its BTAs outweigh the adjustment costs that businesses would incur in order to utilise them. This not only implies that ASEAN will have to simultaneously undertake unilateral liberalisation, but also that implementation integrity is going to be absolutely crucial for the success of its BTAs. This requires effective management of the emerging Asian noodle bowl, as observed by Baldwin (2006). While a guideline for future negotiations involving certain best practices would be helpful in bringing about some consistency among the BTAs,[13] it remains to be seen whether ASEAN can adopt best practices for designing, and implementing BTAs that do end up being the building blocks towards Asian economic integration.

References

Angtkeiwicz, A. and J. Whalley (2005). "BRICSAM and the Non-WTO", Paper presented at the BRICSAM Project Organisational meeting at the Centre for International Governance Innovation (CIGI). May 26-28. Waterloo, Canada.

Asher, M.G and R. Sen (2006). "The Case for Integration between India and the Rest of Asia", presented at the AusAID South Asia Research Facility Conference on *South Asia: Integration or Looking East*. September 25-26.

Asher, M.G. and S. Srivastava (2003). "India and the Asian Economic Community", *RIS Discussion Paper* No. 51. New Delhi: Research and Information System for Developing Countries (RIS).

Baldwin, R. (2006). "Managing the Noodle Bowl: The Fragility of East Asian Regionalism", *Policy Paper*. Geneva: Graduate Institute of International Studies.

———. (1993). "A Domino Theory of Regionalism", *NBER Working Paper* No. 4465. MA: Cambridge.

Banda, O.G.D. and J. Whalley (2005). "Beyond Goods and Services: Competition Policy, Investment, Mutual Recognition, Movement of Natural Persons and Broader Cooperation Provisions of Recent FTAs involving ASEAN Countries", *NBER Working Paper* No. 11232. MA: Cambridge.

Bhagwati, J. (1995). "US Trade Policy: The Infatuation with Free Trade Areas", in *The Dangerous Drift to Preferential Trade Agreements*. Washington DC: The AEI Press.

———. (1993). "Regionalism and Multilateralism: An Overview", in Jamie de Melo and Arvind Panagariya (eds.), *New Dimensions in Regional Integratio*. Cambridge: Cambridge University Press.

Bhagwati, J. and A. Panagariya (eds.) (1996). *The Economics of Preferential Trade Agreements*. Washington DC: AEI Press.

Crawford, J.A. and R.V. Fiorentino (2005). "The Changing Landscape of Regional Trade Agreements", *WTO Discussion Paper* No. 8. Geneva: World Trade Organization.

Hew, D. and R. Sen (2004). "Towards an ASEAN Economics Community: Challenges and Prospects", *ISEAS Working Paper* No. 1. Singapore: Institute of Southeast Asian Studies (ISEAS).

Krueger, A. (1997). "Problems with Overlapping Free Trade Area", in T. Ito and A. Krueger (eds.) *Regionalism versus Multilateral Trade Arrangements*. Chicago: The University of Chicago Press.

Kumar, N. (2006). "Longer-Term Vision of India-ASEAN Partnership: Towards an Asian Economic Community", in Nagesh Kumar, Rahul Sen and Mukul Asher (eds.), *ASEAN-India Economic Relations: Meeting the Challenges of Globalisation*. New Delhi: Research and Information System for Developing Countries (RIS) and Singapore: Institute of Southeast Asian Studies (ISEAS).

13. For Best Practices Guidelines on Asian FTAs, see Plummer (2006).

Kumar, N. (2004). "A Vision of an Asian Economic Community", in Nagesh Kumar (ed.), *Towards an Asian Economic Community: Vision of a New Asia.* New Delhi: Research and Information System for Developing Countries (RIS) and Singapore: Institute of Southeast Asian Studies (ISEAS).

Liang, M. (2005). "Singapore's Trade Policies: Priorities and Options", *ASEAN Economic Bulletin*, Vol. 22(1): 49-59.

Plummer, M. (2006). "Towards Win-Win Regionalism in Asia: Issues and Challenges in Forming Efficient Trade Agreements in Asia", paper presented at the workshop on *Brainstorming on FTAs: Issues and Challenges in Designing Effective Trade Agreements in Asia*, organised by the Asian Development Bank (ADB). Manila. 20 March.

Rajan, R. and R. Sen (2005). "The New Wave of FTAs in Asia: Implications for ASEAN, China and India", in the ADB volume *Asian Economic Cooperation and Integration*. Manila: Asian Development Bank.

Sally, R. and R. Sen (2005). "Whither Trade Policies in Southeast Asia? The Wider Asian and Global Context", *ASEAN Economic Bulletin*, Vol. 22(1), pp.92-115 (Also reprinted in Bibek Debroy and Debashis Chakraborty (eds.), *The Trade Game: Negotiation Trends at WTO and Concerns of Developing Countries*. New Delhi: Academic Foundation in association with Liberty Institute and Rajiv Gandhi Institute of Contemporary Studies, 2006.

Sen, R. (2005). "The Emerging Wave of New Regionalism in Asia: A Comparative Analysis of Regional Trading Agreements in ASEAN, China and India", Paper presented at the Venice Summer 2005 Workshop on *Global Economic Negotiations* organised by CESIfo. 20-21 July. Venice, Italy: Venice International University.

Severino, R. (2005). "Framing the ASEAN Charter: An ISEAS Perspective". Singapore: Institute of Southeast Asian Studies (ISEAS).

United Nations (2005). *UN-Comtrade Database*.

Winters, A. (1998). "Regionalism and the Next Round", in Jeffrey Schott (ed.), *Launching New Global Trade Talks: An Action Agenda*. Washington DC: Institute for International Economics (IIE).

6

Progress of ASEAN Initiatives for Investment and Services Cooperation

Implications for Wider Regional Economic Integration in Asia

WISARN PUPPHAVESA and SASATRA SUDSAWASD

Progress of ASEAN Initiatives for Investment Cooperation

At the fifth ASEAN Summit in Bangkok in December 1995, the ASEAN leaders decided to establish the ASEAN Investment Area (AIA) to attract foreign direct investment (FDI) from outside as well as within the ASEAN region. Later, in November 1996, at the informal ASEAN Economic Ministers' Meeting in Manila, it was agreed to achieve AIA by 2010. A task force was set up to draft the framework agreement on the AIA, which was then signed by the ASEAN economic ministers on 7 October, 1998. The Agreement has been in force since 7 April, 1999. Cambodia joined on 30 April, 1999, thus extending the AIA across all 10 ASEAN countries

The objectives of the Framework Agreement on AIA are:

a) To establish a competitive ASEAN Investment Area with a more liberal transparent investment environment amongst member states in order to increase FDI inflows from both ASEAN and non-ASEAN sources into ASEAN, jointly promote ASEAN as the most attractive investment area, strengthen and increase the competitiveness of ASEAN's economic sectors, reduce or eliminate regulations and conditions which impede investment flows and the operation of investment projects in ASEAN; and

b) To contribute towards free flow of investments by 2020.[1]

1. *http://www.aseansec. org/7994.htm*

Member states are obliged to undertake the cooperation and facilitation programme (Schedule I), the promotion and awareness programme (Schedule II) and the liberalisation programme (Schedule III). Under Schedule I, member states are required to take:

a) individual initiatives to increase transparency of investment rules, regulations, policies and procedures, simplify and expedite procedures for applications and approvals of investment projects, and expand the number of bilateral Double Taxation Avoidance Agreements among ASEAN member states; and

b) collective initiatives to establish a database for ASEAN Supporting Industries and ASEAN Technology Supplies and a database on ASEAN investment and opportunities, promote public-private sector linkages through regular dialogues with the ASEAN business community and other international organisations to identify investment impediments within and outside ASEAN and propose ways to improve the ASEAN investment environment, identify target areas for technical cooperation such as human resource development (HRD), infrastructure, supporting industries, small and medium enterprises (SMEs), information technoloty (IT), research and development (R&D), etc. review and improve the ASEAN Agreement for the Promotion and Protection of Investment, and examine the possibility of an ASEAN Double Taxation Agreement.

Under Schedule II, member states must agree to organise joint investment promotion activities, conduct regular consultation among investment agencies of ASEAN on investment promotion matters, organise investment-related training programmes for officials of investment agencies of ASEAN, exchange lists of promoted sectors/ industries where investment from other member states may be encouraged and initiate promotional activities and examine ways to support promotion efforts of other member states.

Under Schedule III, member states are required to:

a) unilaterally reduce and eliminate restrictive investment measures and liberalise rules, regulations and policies relating to investment, rules on licensing conditions, rules relating to access to domestic finance and rules to facilitate payment, receipts and repatriation of profits by investors;

b) undertake individual action plans to open up all industries for investment to ASEAN investors by 2010 and to all investors by 2020, to extend national treatment to all ASEAN investors by 2010 and to all investors by 2020; and

c) promote freer flow of capital, skilled labour, professionals and technology among ASEAN member states.

Note, however, that Article 7 of the Agreement stipulates that member states immediately open all their industries for investment and accord national treatment to ASEAN investors subject to exceptions under the Temporary Exclusion List (TEL) and the Sensitive List (SL). The TEL would be reviewed every two years and would be progressively phased out by 2010 by all member states except Vietnam, Lao PDR and Myanmar. Vietnam would phase out its TEL by 2013 and Lao PDR and Myanmar by 2015. The SL would be reviewed by 1 January, 2003 and periodically thereafter as decided by the AIA Council.

A member state is required to extend preferential treatment, under any existing or future agreements to which it is a party, to all other member states on the most favoured nation (MFN) basis.

The Agreement also calls for transparency in the member states' relevant measures, laws, regulations and administrative guidelines pertaining to or affecting this agreement and including those international agreements pertaining to or affecting investment to which the member states are also signatories. (Article II).

Certain exceptions are provided in the interest of national security, public morals, human, animal or plant life, health, prevention of deceptive and fraudulent practices, protection of the privacy of individuals and the equitable and effective imposition and collection of direct taxes with respect to investments or the investors of member states.

In addition, emergency safeguard measures and measures to safeguard the balance of payments are allowed for member states to prevent or to remedy any serious injury and threat resulting from implementation of the liberalisation programme or in the event of serious balance of payments and external financial difficulties or threat.

It may be observed that under the Agreement, member states unilaterally draw up and implement their own liberalisation plans in accordance with the Agreement. The preferential treatment is then extended on MFN basis amongst those member states that meet the requirements in the Agreement. The member state that is not ready to make the required concessions would have to waive its right to such concessions extended by other member states unless the counterpart member state is willing to forego the waiver. This mechanism is the well-known ASEAN-X which was employed in the ASEAN Free Trade Agreement (AFTA).

One noteworthy feature of the Framework Agreement on AIA is the provision of preferential differential treatment for less developed new members of ASEAN which are allowed to take 3-5 years longer to achieve the liberalisation target but can get access to other member states' MFN concessions during the period.

At the sixth ASEAN Summit on 16 December, 1998, the ASEAN leaders agreed to adopt bold measures in order to revive the ASEAN economies from the ongoing economic and financial crisis. The TEL for the manufacturing sector would be phased out by 2003 by all member states except Cambodia, Lao PDR and Vietnam, which would do so no later than 2010. In addition the First AIA Council Meeting on 5 March, 1999 agreed to widen and elaborate AIA coverage to include manufacturing, agriculture, fishery, forestry, mining and quarrying and services incidental to these sectors. These were then undertaken by the Protocol to Amend the Framework Agreement on the AIA agreed in September 2001.

Subsequently, it was reported that the AIA process has made good progress. At the sixth AIA Ministerial Council Meeting in September 2003, it was reported that member states had opened up more industries and granted more investment measures to foreign investment by phasing in the list of sectors and investment measures in the TEL. Significant achievements had also been made in transferring sectors and measures in the SL to the TEL. Member states also, on individual basis, introduced more favourable measures to improve their investment regime. Several projects on investment promotion and facilitation aiming at strengthening capacity building on regional integration, improving transparency and harmonisation and improving FDI data quality were implemented successfully with support from dialogue partners and international organisations such as United Nations Conference on Trade and Development (UNCTAD). To enhance transparency and promote greater awareness of the ASEAN investment environment, the Council agreed to publish an updated Compendium of Investment Policy Measures and the FDI data set. The Council also agreed to have regular dialogue with ASEAN partners to spearhead investment cooperation as well as to have more active dialogue with ASEAN and non-ASEAN business representatives. Recognising the growing importance of the services sector, the Council agreed to work out the scope of expanding the AIA to include services, namely, education services, healthcare, telecommunication, tourism, banking and finance, insurance, trading, e-commerce, distribution and logistics, transportation and warehousing, and professional services such as accounting, engineering and advertising.

In the following year, 2004, progress was made in the area of promotion of awareness of development in ASEAN's supporting industries and understanding of transnational corporations' strategies. Some member countries have reviewed and submitted the revised TEL and SL.

The ASEAN Business Advisory Council (ABAC) in cooperation with the Coordinating Committee on Investments (CCI) successfully organised and concluded the First ASEAN Business and Investment Summit in Bali in October 2003. The first CCI-Japan Investment Consultation was also held in May 2004. Continued progress in the AIA process would be made through enhancing external linkages with dialogue partners and joint consultations with the private sector. It was also agreed that ASEAN's investment and trade policies should work in tandem to ensure ASEAN's competitiveness.

Another big step in ASEAN's initiatives in investment cooperation was taken when the ASEAN Framework Agreement for the Integration of Priority Sectors was signed on 29 November, 2004 to accelerate the integration of priority sectors and realise the end goal of the ASEAN

Economic Community which the ASEAN leaders agreed to establish by 2020. The Agreement identified 11 sectors, namely, agro-based products, air transport, automotives, e-ASEAN, electronics, fisheries, healthcare, rubber-based products, textiles and apparels, tourism and wood-based products as the priority sectors. The Agreement provides for liberalisation of trade in goods, trade in services and investment, trade and investment facilitation as well as promotion and monitoring in the priority sectors. The Agreement also includes other areas for integration, such as intellectual property rights cooperation, industrial complementation promotion and human resource development among ASEAN member states.

On liberalisation of trade in goods, all the Common Effective Preferential Tariff (CEPT)—AFTA tariffs on priority sector products would be eliminated by 1 January, 2007 for ASEAN-6 and by January 2012 for Cambodia, Lao PDR, Myanmar and Vietnam (CLMV) (with certain exception). Member states would establish the database of ASEAN Non-tariff Measures (NTMs) by 30 June, 2004, establish criteria to identify NTMs that are barriers to trade by 30 June, 2005, establish a definitive work programme for the removal of such NTMs by 31 December, 2005, and adopt the WTO Agreement on Import Licensing Procedures and develop common implementation guidelines appropriate for ASEAN by 31 December, 2004. Member states would also endeavour to expand the coverage of the ASEAN Integration System of Preferences (AISP) Scheme by including products in the priority sectors.

As for trade in services, member states would set clear targets and schedules for progressive liberalisation for each round of negotiations toward achieving freer flow of trade in services earlier than 2020, accelerate the service liberalisation for the priority sectors by 2010, accelerate the development of Mutual Recognition Arrangements (MRAs) by 1 January, 2008 and promote joint ventures and cooperation, including third-country markets, based on the ASEAN-X mechanism.

Regarding investment, member states would accelerate the opening up of sectors currently in the SL by transferring them to the TEL under the AIA, using the ASEAN-X formula, beginning 2004, reduce restrictive investment measures in the SL beginning 2004 and complete

...ation of restr... investment measures in the TEL by 31 ...ember, 2010 for A...N-6, by 2013 for Vietnam and by 2015 for Cambodia, Lao PDR ... Myanmar. They would identify programme and activities to pro... investment in ASEAN by 31 December, 2005, promote manu...ring processes in ASEAN to take advantage of their comparativ... ...gths through establishment of a network of ASEAN free trade zones to facilitate outsourcing beginning 2005 and undertake more efficient joint ASEAN facilitation and promotion measures to promote FDI on ongoing basis. They would also promote and facilitate joint/cross border investments in manufacturing activities. The CLMV member states would provide special investment incentive where appropriate for FDI from ASEAN-6 while ASEAN-6 would implement special measures to promote and facilitate relocation of investment to CLMV especially for labour intensive manufacturing activities. Regarding trade and investment facilitation, member states would improve the CEPT Rules of Origin by making them more transparent, predictable and standardised and adopting substantial transformation as an alternative criterion for origin status, apply the ASEAN Harmonised Tariff Nomenclature (AHTN) for extra-ASEAN trade on an ongoing basis and simplify, improve and harmonise custom declaration forms by 31 December, 2005. They would ensure the Green Lane System for CEPT products by 31 December, 2004, develop the Single Window approach including the electronic processing of trade documents at national and regional level by 31 December, 2005, develop common implementation guidelines by December 2004 to fulfil the obligations of the WTO Agreement on Customs Valuation. Member states would take steps to accelerate the development of MRAs and harmonise product standards and technical regulations, expedite the development of integrated transport logistics services within ASEAN and accelerate completion of MRAs to facilitate the movement of business persons, experts, professionals, skilled labour and talents.

On trade and investment promotion, member states would intensify joint intra-ASEAN and extra-ASEAN trade promotion efforts, assist CLMV in organising promotional activities, undertake more effective joint ASEAN facilitation and promotion measures and develop new sources of inward FDI, such as China, India and Korea.

The Agreement also provides that member states expand the scope of ASEAN intellectual property rights cooperation to include cooperation in copyright information exchanges and enforcement. It expects member states to promote industrial complementation among ASEAN manufacturers through identification and development of specialisation of production processes, R&D and testing facilities based on comparative advantage of individual member states and development of guidelines on promotion of outsourcing arrangements among themselves. They must also cooperate to develop and upgrade skills and capacity building.

ASEAN Initiatives in Trade in Services

ASEAN cooperation in services was launched through the signing of the ASEAN Framework Agreement on Services (AFAS) on 15 December, 1995 by ASEAN Economic Ministers during the fifth ASEAN Summit in Bangkok.

The AFAS is intended to improve the efficiency and competitiveness of ASEAN services suppliers through elimination of restriction to trade in services. It provides broad guidelines for member countries to improve market access and ensure national treatment for services suppliers among ASEAN countries in all four modes of services supply. It also provides rules for related aspects such as mutual recognition, dispute settlements, institutional mechanism and other areas of cooperation in services. The commitments of liberalisation under AFAS is consistent with but beyond member countries' commitment under GATS (GATS-plus). ASEAN has made good progress in negotiations to achieve the objective of the AFAS. Four packages of services commitments have been concluded covering the following services sectors:

- air transport including sales and marketing of air transport services, computer reservation, aircraft repair and maintenance, etc.;
- business services including IT services, accounting, auditing, legal, architecture, engineering, market research, etc.;
- construction including construction of commercial buildings, civil engineering, installation works, rental of construction equipments, etc.;

- financial services including banking, insurance, securities and broking, financial advisory, consumer finance, etc.;
- maritime transport including international passenger and freight transport, storage and warehousing, etc.;
- telecommunication including public telephone services, mobile phone services, business networks services, data and message transmission, etc.; and
- tourism including hotel and lodging services, food serving, tour operator, travel agency, etc.

ASEAN countries continue to expand the negotiations to cover all sectors and all modes of supply to achieve free flow of services by 2020.

With regard to liberalisation, the Agreement calls for substantial elimination of all existing discriminatory measures and market access limitations amongst member countries and prohibits new or more discriminatory measures and market access limitations.

Negotiations on MRAs are in progress in a number of areas including engineering, architecture, accountancy, surveying and tourism.

The Agreement provides for cooperation efforts in service sectors through the establishment or improvement of infrastructural facilities, joint production, marketing and purchasing arrangements, R&D and exchange of information.

Implications for Wider Regional Economic Integration in Asia

Widening of ASEAN integration by accession of CLMV to AFTA will increase the extent of trade complementarity amongst ASEAN countries thus enhancing the trade creation effect and reducing the scope and extent of the trade diversion effect. Larger membership will increase the opportunities for efficiency gain from economies of scale for member countries. CLMV accession, moreover, helps facilitate structural adjustment through industrial relocation in the ASEAN region.

Deepening integration through investment and services liberalisation and cooperation will not only facilitate the structural adjustment of ASEAN as mentioned above and improve efficiency in production and trade overall but will also induce more investment that boost dynamic effect of regional integration. ASEAN could, therefore, be more efficient and competitive to create better economic growth and development prospects which would, through the income effect, increase trade and investment relations with other countries in Asia and outside Asia. There might be some substitution effect on trade and crowding out effect on investment on non-ASEAN countries in Asia. However, competition need not always imply substitution between producers of ASEAN and non-ASEAN countries. To some extent competition might turn into product differentiation and thus increase intra-industry trade and investment in ASEAN and non-ASEAN countries.

The extent of these effects depends on the economic structures of the economies involved and the coverage and depth of ASEAN integration. It is observed that ASEAN investment and services liberalisation is based on the ASEAN-X formula which limits the opportunities to realise potential efficiency gains and which might not effectively induce desirable restructuring and investment. Moreover, the depth and pace of investment and services liberalisation is quite modest and thus might lack effectiveness. Also, to a large extent, the cooperation is dependent on government action which tends to move slowly in practice. Consequently, the implied effect on non-ASEAN countries of Asia might not be of great significance. The effect could be larger and induce stronger integration for the whole Asian region, should the ASEAN investment and services cooperation be open more to non-ASEAN investors and services providers and ASEAN member states be more willing to collectively liberalise their investment and services.

Impact of ASEAN Integration on FDI Flows to Other Asian Economies

Methodology

Given the already discussed widening and deepening of ASEAN integration, the impact on wider regional economic integration in Asia would depend on the nature of trade and investment relationship within ASEAN and between ASEAN and the rest of Asian region. Various empirical studies based on the well known gravity model (for example, Frankel *et al.*, 1995; Sudsawasd and Mongsawad, 2005) find consistent results that trade flows tend to rise with the greater potential demand and the greater potential supply; while it tends to fall with the longer distance between trading countries. These results imply that wider and deeper ASEAN integration through the Initiatives for Investment and Services Cooperation would tend to also enhance trade between ASEAN and other Asian economies.

Recently, the gravity model has been extended to investigate bilateral FDI flows. Eichengreen and Tong (2005) used the gravity model to assess the impact of China's FDI inflows on other countries' FDI. Sudsawasd and Chaisrisawatsuk (2005) used a similar approach to assess the effects of the rising of trade and FDI of China and India on ASEAN-5 economies.[2]

In this section, the focus is on the heightening of ASEAN integration as a destination of FDI. The aim of this study is to seek the answer for the following questions. Which Asian economies have observed FDI inflows diverted toward ASEAN? This would be the case when those economies are substituted with ASEAN in terms of FDI destination. On the other hand, which Asian economies are more attractive to FDI inflows as ASEAN becomes more attractive as the destination for FDI? This would be the case if ASEAN and those countries are part of the same investment networks in which the FDI in those two destinations are complementary.

The empirical framework of this study is to employ the modification of the standard gravity model of bilateral FDI, which is augmented by adding total ASEAN-5 FDI receipts from the same source, namely, OECD (Organisation for Economic Cooperation and Development) countries, as the parameter of interest. Then, two types of model specifications are estimated. In the first specification, this study examines the effects of levels of FDI inflows toward ASEAN-5 on levels of other countries' FDI inflows, in US dollar values. Next, the second specification is to determine whether a recent increase in FDI

2. ASEAN-5 countries are Indonesia, Malaysia, Philippines, Singapore and Thailand.

to GDP (gross domestic product) ratio in increases or decreases FDI to GDP ratio of other recipient countries.

Thus, the first model is specified as:

$$\ln(FDI_{ijt}) = \beta_0 + \beta_1 \ln(FDI_{iASEAN5t}) + \beta_2 \ln(GDP_{it}) + \beta_3 \ln(GDP_{jt})$$
$$+\beta_4 \ln(GDPPC_{it}) + \beta_5 \ln(GDPPC_{jt}) + \beta_6 \ln(DIST_{ij}) + \beta_7 Landl_{ijt} + \varepsilon_{ijt}.$$

And the second model is:

$$\ln(FDI_{ijt} / GDP_{jt}) = \beta_0 + \beta_1 \ln(FDI_{iASEAN5t} / GDP_{ASEAN5t}) + \beta_2 \ln(GDP_{it}) + \beta_3 \ln(GDP_{jt})$$
$$+\beta_4 \ln(GDPPC_{it}) + \beta_5 \ln(GDPPC_{jt}) + \beta_6 \ln(DIST_{ij}) + \beta_7 Landl_{ijt} + \varepsilon_{ijt}.$$

Where i and j denote source and recipient countries; t denotes time.

FDI = real bilateral FDI outflows from source i to recipient j,
GDP = real GDP,
GDPPC = real GDP per capita,
DIST = distance between source i and recipient j,
Landl = number of landlocked countries (0, 1, or 2).

The scope of this study is limited to only FDI outflows from 30 OECD countries to 59 OECD and non-OECD countries over the period 1980-2003.[3] The data of FDI, GDP, and GDP per capita are converted to constant US$ 2000. The data are taken from the World Bank's *World Development Indicators*, Andrew Rose (2005) dataset, and the Source OECD.

The dataset is an unbalanced panel. Several econometric issues usually presented in panel data include serial correlation and heteroscedasticity. To remedy these problems, the White covariance matrix estimator is employed to produce the robust standard error. In addition, there is the potential endogeneity of ASEAN-5 FDI receipts. The standard treatment of this problem is to introduce instrumental variables that are exogenous and strongly correlated with ASEAN-5

3. The 30 OECD countries are Australia, Austria, Belgium, Canada, Czech Republic, Denmark, Finland, France, Germany, Greece, Hungary, Iceland, Ireland, Italy, Japan, Korea, Luxembourg, Mexico, Netherlands, New Zealand, Norway, Poland, Portugal, Slovak Republic, Spain, Sweden, Switzerland, Turkey, United Kingdom and United States.

FDI. The instruments chosen in this study are GDP and GDP per capita of ASEAN-5. Hence, two different forms of panel data estimator are estimated: the standard random effect model with the robust standard error and the random effect model with the instrumental variables (IV).

The models are regressed by using both aggregated data of all recipient countries and disaggregated data of each individual FDI recipient country as one might argue that the effects or the estimated coefficients would be different. However, as stated, the objective of this section is to analyse only the impact on Asian economies. Therefore, only disaggregated data of seven Asian countries are estimated here. These seven countries are Australia, China, Hong Kong, India, Japan, Korea and New Zealand. Tables 6.1-6.8 report all estimation results. In each table, the first two columns show coefficient estimates for the first specification; while the results from the second specification are contained in the last two columns.

Empirical Results

Regression Using Levels of FDI Inflows

For the full aggregated data, the estimated signs of most standard gravity coefficients are as expected. Larger sources of FDI countries, as indicated by larger GDP_i, have more resources to invest abroad and appear to be more attractive destinations for FDI. So they are likely to engage more in bilateral FDI. For the distance variables, countries located at a greater distance are less likely to engage in bilateral FDI, while the landlocked countries have a positive impact.

However, the results are somewhat surprising for the coefficients on GDP per capita. Source countries with higher GDP per capita appear to be less likely to engage in FDI. This could mean that richer countries tend to concentrate on investing at home more than they invest abroad. The results also suggest that as recipients of FDI are wealthier, measured by higher $GDPPC_j$, they become less attractive for FDI. This could imply that countries with higher GDP per capita may reflect higher costs to invest. Hence, multinational companies may look for other countries that have lower costs and are more attractive for FDI.

The estimated coefficient of parameter interest, $FDI_{i\,ASEAN5}$, is insignificant in the standard random effect model, but it turns out to be significant with the IV instruments. The results confirm conventional wisdom that an increase in FDI inflows to ASEAN-5 is certainly due to FDI diverting from other FDI recipients. That is, ASEAN-5 is a substitute of other FDI recipients. A one percentage point increase in the level of FDI in ASEAN-5 leads to about 1.02 percentage point reduction in the level of FDI to other recipient countries.

For the disaggregated data, coefficients become less significant. The effects of FDI inflows toward ASEAN-5 can be categorised into two groups. In the first group, when FDI inflows toward ASEAN-5 increase, the dollar amounts of FDI inflows toward Australia and New Zealand also increase. This may suggest that ASEAN-5, Australia and New Zealand are in the same investment chains. And FDI in those countries are, indeed, complementary to each other.

The opposite results are found in the second group consisting five Asian countries—China, Hong Kong, India, Japan and Korea. These countries observe FDI inflows actually diverted toward ASEAN-5 countries. In other words, they compete for FDI from the same source OECD countries. In this case, FDI in ASEAN-5 and those five Asian countries can be regarded as substitution.

Regression Using Ratios of FDI Inflows to GDP

In the second specification, this study uses ratios of FDI inflows to GDP of a recipient country as the dependent variable. And now the variable of interest is the ratio of ASEAN-5's FDI inflows to GDP. Note that the results obtained from the standard random effects estimator and the random effects with instruments estimator are quite similar. Therefore, only results from the standard random effects estimator are analysed throughout the remainder of this section.

Our major findings indicate that an increase in the proportion of FDI receipts to GDP of ASEAN-5 significantly increases other recipients' ratio as well. For a full sample data, a one percentage point increase in the ratio of ASEAN-5's FDI to GDP causes other countries' FDI to GDP ratios to increase by about 0.34 percentage points. When disaggregate data of each of the seven Asian countries are used, the effects of the ratio of ASEAN-5's FDI to GDP substantially vary among Asian countries. For example, the effect on New Zealand is more than 50 times larger than the effect on Korea. Likewise, the effect on Australia is equal to that on Hong Kong. Nonetheless, the estimated signs for each country are all positive.

The signs of gravity coefficients are consistent with those in the first specification, confirming underlying hypotheses. One exception is that the sign of the coefficient on GDP_j changes to a negative sign, where it needs to be reinterpreted with care. As GDP of recipient countries increase, it certainly ensures that the ratio of FDI to GDP of recipient countries must decrease assuming no change in levels of FDI. Thus, the negative sign is expected. Unless an increase in the level of FDI is larger than the level of GDP increase, under this circumstance, the sign of GDP_j variable would become positive, where it does not appear to be the case here.

Conclusion

Our empirical findings suggest that the existing nature of investment relations between ASEAN and other Asian economies tend to be complementary rather than substitute. Hence, the ASEAN Initiatives for Investment Cooperation and Trade in Services, while increase trade and investment within ASEAN, could also increase trade between ASEAN and other Asian economies as well as increase FDI in most other Asian economies. The wider and deeper could the Asian economies integrate through market mechanism should the ASEAN integration be deepened and effective.

Table 6.1

Gravity Model Regression Results

(i=30 OECD Countries; j=All FDI Recipient Countries)

Variable	*Dep. Var. ln(FDIij)*		*Dep. Var. ln(FDIij/GDPj)*	
	Random Effect	*IV*	*Random Effect*	*IV*
$\ln(FDI_{iASEAN5})$	-0.0004 (0.01)	-1.0210 *** (0.18)		
$\ln(FDI_{iASEAN5}/GDP_{ASEAN5})$			0.3482 *** (0.02)	1.2344 *** (0.02)
$\ln GDP_i$	0.8892 *** (0.01)	0.6601 *** (0.02)	0.8511 *** (0.01)	0.7349 *** (0.01)
$\ln GDP_j$	0.9732 *** (0.00)	0.8542 *** (0.00)	-0.0381 *** (0.00)	-0.0745 *** (0.00)
$\ln GDPPC_i$	-1.1575 *** (0.02)	-0.3687 *** (0.02)	-0.9609 *** (0.02)	-0.4759 *** (0.02)
$\ln GDPPC_j$	-1.1635 *** (0.01)	-0.4880 *** (0.01)	-0.9388 *** (0.02)	-0.3807 *** (0.02)
$\ln Dist$	-0.3904 *** (0.03)	-0.1812 *** (0.02)	-0.3496 *** (0.03)	-0.2480 *** (0.03)
Landl	1.2937 *** (0.07)	0.9880 *** (0.04)	1.2744 *** (0.06)	1.1973 *** (0.07)
Constant	-0.4441 (0.51)	16.6041 *** (3.61)	1.2649 *** (0.44)	-5.0934 *** (0.48)
R^2	0.4883	0.5694	0.1151	0.1043
No. of Obs.	11231	11231	11231	11231

Note: ***, **, * denote 1 per cent, 5 per cent, 10 per cent significant levels, respectively. Robust standard errors are in parentheses.

Source:
- FDI is the foreign direct investment measured in constant 2000 US dollars with data obtained from the Source OECD website *(www.sourceoecd.org)*.
- GDP is measured in constant 2000 US dollars with data obtained from the *World Development Indicator 2005 CD-Rom*. GDPPC is per capita GDP measured in constant 2000 U.S. dollars with data obtained from the *World Development Indicator 2005 CD-Rom*.
- The DIST and Landl variables, data are obtained from the Andrew Rose (2005) dataset.

Table 6.2

Gravity Model Regression Results

(i=30 OECD Countries; j=Australia)

Variable	*Dep. Var. ln(FDIij)*		*Dep. Var. ln(FDIij/GDPj)*	
	Random Effect	*IV*	*Random Effect*	*IV*
$\ln(FDI_{iASEAN5})$	0.0257 (0.02)	2.0569 *** (2.95)		
$\ln(FDI_{iASEAN5}/GDP_{ASEAN5})$			0.0999 *** (0.04)	0.7419 *** (0.14)
$\ln GDP_i$	0.0006 (0.01)	-0.1911 (0.29)	-0.0013 (0.01)	-0.0631 *** (0.02)
$\ln GDP_j$	0.0365 (0.08)	-0.8702 (1.38)	-0.9722 *** (0.07)	-1.0518 *** (0.16)
$\ln GDPPC_i$	-0.0027 (0.01)	-0.2285 (0.34)	-0.0056 (0.01)	-0.0690 ** (0.03)
$\ln GDPPC_j$	-1.5927 *** (0.07)	-1.1122 (0.81)	-1.3786 *** (0.11)	0.1819 (0.37)
ln*Dist*	0.0014 (0.03)	0.6312 (0.93)	0.0204 (0.02)	0.2276 *** (0.07)
Landl	-0.0173 (0.02)	-0.3625 (0.53)	-0.0227 * (0.01)	-0.1272 ** (0.06)
Constant	38.3558 *** (1.69)	13.9820 (37.52)	41.5524 *** (1.81)	28.6083 *** (4.87)
R^2	0.8513	0.1140	0.9119	0.6090
No. of Obs.	245	245	245	245

Note: ***, **, * denote 1 per cent, 5 per cent, 10 per cent significant levels, respectively. Robust standard errors are in parentheses

Source: Same as Table 6.1

Table 6.3

Gravity Model Regression Results

(i=30 OECD Countries; j=China)

Variable	*Dep. Var. ln(FDIij)*		*Dep. Var. ln(FDIij/GDPj)*	
	Random Effect	*IV*	*Random Effect*	*IV*
$\ln(FDI_{iASEAN5})$	0.0130 (0.01)	-0.2348 *** (0.18)		
$\ln(FDI_{iASEAN5}/GDP_{ASEAN5})$			0.0214 ** (0.01)	2.1256 (2.84)
$\ln GDP_i$	0.0040 (0.00)	0.0239 (0.02)	0.0032 (0.00)	-0.1858 (0.26)
$\ln GDP_j$	0.8893 *** (0.05)	0.8240 *** (0.07)	-0.1184 ** (0.05)	-0.7319 (0.91)
$\ln GDPPC_i$	-0.0018 (0.01)	0.0151 (0.02)	-0.0028 (0.01)	-0.2529 (0.35)
$\ln GDPPC_j$	-1.2846 *** (0.04)	-1.2456 *** (0.05)	-1.2672 *** (0.04)	0.3786 (2.24)
$\ln Dist$	-0.0099 (0.01)	-0.0390 (0.03)	-0.0087 (0.01)	0.2914 (0.42)
Landl	-0.0015 (0.01)	0.0252 (0.04)	-0.0026 (0.01)	-0.2804 (0.40)
Constant	7.8729 *** (1.28)	14.5257 *** (4.93)	12.8847 *** (1.27)	23.7236 (17.26)
R^2	0.9533	0.8883	0.9813	0.3427
No. of Obs.	220	220	220	220

Note: ***, **, * denote 1 per cent, 5 per cent, 10 per cent significant levels, respectively. Robust standard errors are in parentheses.

Source: Same as Table 6.1.

Table 6.4

Gravity Model Regression Results

(i=30 OECD Countries; j=Hong Kong)

Variable	*Dep. Var. ln(FDIij)*		*Dep. Var. ln(FDIij/GDPj)*	
	Random Effect	*IV*	*Random Effect*	*IV*
$\ln(FDI_{iASEAN5})$	0.0577 *** (0.02)	-3.9347 *** (4.26)		
$\ln(FDI_{iASEAN5}/GDP_{ASEAN5})$			0.1019 *** (0.03)	1.0478 *** (0.37)
$\ln GDP_i$	0.0044 (0.01)	0.3681 (0.39)	0.0004 (0.01)	-0.0852 ** (0.04)
$\ln GDP_j$	-0.7113 *** (0.19)	2.8689 (4.26)	-1.7322 *** (0.19)	-2.4060 *** (0.55)
$\ln GDPPC_i$	-0.0273 ** (0.01)	0.4151 (0.50)	-0.0325 *** (0.01)	-0.1402 ** (0.06)
$\ln GDPPC_j$	-0.9145 *** (0.20)	-4.8895 (4.70)	-0.7270 *** (0.22)	1.5461 (1.03)
$\ln Dist$	0.0003 (0.02)	-0.7935 (0.87)	0.0102 (0.02)	0.2089 ** (0.09)
Landl	0.0057 (0.02)	0.5932 (0.68)	-0.0008 (0.02)	-0.1392 (0.09)
Constant	50.5999 *** (2.82)	80.4692 * (43.30)	55.2126 *** (2.84)	51.2774 *** (7.60)
R^2	0.8918	0.0336	0.9589	0.7316
No. of Obs.	250	250	250	250

Note: ***, **, * denote 1 per cent, 5 per cent, 10 per cent significant levels, respectively. Robust standard errors are in parentheses.

Source: Same as Table 6.1.

Table 6.5

Gravity Model Regression Results

(i=30 OECD Countries; j=India)

Variable	*Dep. Var. ln(FDIij)*		*Dep. Var. ln(FDIij/GDPj)*	
	Random Effect	*IV*	*Random Effect*	*IV*
$\ln(FDI_{iASEAN5})$	0.0025 (0.01)	-0.3835 *** (0.27)		
$\ln(FDI_{iASEAN5}/GDP_{ASEAN5})$			0.0091 *** (0.01)	0.4420 (0.36)
$\ln GDP_i$	0.0005 (0.00)	0.0363 (0.03)	-0.0001 (0.00)	-0.0388 (0.03)
$\ln GDP_j$	0.5219 *** (0.02)	0.5107 *** (0.06)	-0.4820 *** (0.02)	-0.6623 *** (0.17)
$\ln GDPPC_i$	-0.0056 ** (0.00)	0.0335 (0.03)	-0.0062 ** (0.00)	-0.0484 (0.04)
$\ln GDPPC_j$	-1.7098 *** (0.01)	-1.7158 *** (0.06)	-1.7004 *** (0.02)	-1.2566 *** (0.38)
$\ln Dist$	0.0073 (0.01)	0.0347 (0.04)	0.0066 (0.01)	-0.0351 (0.06)
Landl	-0.0027 (0.00)	0.0474 (0.04)	-0.0035 (0.00)	-0.0564 (0.05)
Constant	20.4840 *** (0.54)	27.9067 *** (5.51)	25.2198 *** (0.55)	29.1471 *** (4.01)
R^2	0.9965	0.9264	0.9922	0.8165
No. of Obs.	235	235	235	235

Note: ***, **, * denote 1 per cent, 5 per cent, 10 per cent significant levels, respectively. Robust standard errors are in parentheses.

Source: Same as Table 6.1.

Table 6.6

Gravity Model Regression Results

(i=30 OECD Countries; j=Japan)

Variable	*Dep. Var. ln(FDIij)*		*Dep. Var. ln(FDIij/GDPj)*	
	Random Effect	*IV*	*Random Effect*	*IV*
$\ln(FDI_{iASEAN5})$	0.0080 (0.02)	-0.3267 *** (0.30)		
$\ln(FDI_{iASEAN5}/GDP_{ASEAN5})$			0.0078 *** (0.02)	-0.0653 (0.06)
$\ln GDP_i$	0.0086 *** (0.00)	0.0329 (0.02)	0.0086 *** (0.00)	0.0139 *** (0.01)
$\ln GDP_j$	-0.0355 ** (0.02)	-0.0474 (0.05)	-1.0369 *** (0.02)	-1.0267 *** (0.02)
$\ln GDPPC_i$	0.0007 (0.00)	0.0226 (0.02)	0.0006 (0.00)	0.0062 (0.01)
$\ln GDPPC_j$	-0.3664 *** (0.06)	-0.3176 ** (0.15)	-0.3425 *** (0.09)	-0.5546 *** (0.18)
ln*Dist*	0.0012 (0.00)	-0.0040 (0.01)	0.0013 (0.00)	-0.0009 (0.01)
Landl	0.0105 ** (0.01)	0.0501 (0.04)	0.0105 ** (0.01)	0.0193 (0.01)
Constant	28.6020 *** (0.54)	35.1102 *** (5.84)	33.1734 *** (0.59)	34.9314 *** (1.47)
R^2	0.6182	0.1193	0.9862	0.9824
No. of Obs.	227	227	227	227

Note: ***, **, * denote 1 per cent, 5 per cent, 10 per cent significant levels, respectively. Robust standard errors are in parentheses.

Source: Same as Table 6.1.

Table 6.7

Gravity Model Regression Results
(i=30 OECD Countries; j=Korea)

Variable	*Dep. Var. ln(FDIij)*		*Dep. Var. ln(FDIij/GDPj)*	
	Random Effect	*IV*	*Random Effect*	*IV*
$\ln(FDI_{iASEAN5})$	-0.0066 (0.01)	-1.0295 *** (0.78)		
$\ln(FDI_{iASEAN5}/GDP_{ASEAN5})$			0.0040 *** (0.01)	1.3674 (2.13)
$\ln GDP_i$	0.0007 (0.00)	0.0811 (0.06)	-0.0002 (0.00)	-0.1065 (0.17)
$\ln GDP_j$	0.2057 *** (0.01)	0.3843 ** (0.18)	-0.7961 *** (0.01)	-1.0170 *** (0.38)
$\ln GDPPC_i$	-0.0003 (0.00)	0.0642 (0.07)	-0.0009 (0.00)	-0.0849 (0.15)
$\ln GDPPC_j$	-1.0172 *** (0.01)	-1.1730 *** (0.17)	-1.0120 *** (0.01)	0.4380 (2.27)
ln*Dist*	-0.0080 * (0.00)	-0.2081 (0.16)	-0.0059 (0.00)	0.2611 (0.42)
Landl	0.0002 (0.01)	0.1251 (0.12)	-0.0011 (0.01)	-0.1676 (0.28)
Constant	28.2354 *** (0.30)	46.7095 *** (14.21)	32.7043 *** (0.27)	26.5561 *** (10.13)
R^2	0.9877	0.4545	0.9969	0.6589
No. of Obs.	234	234	234	234

Notes: ***, **, * denote 1 per cent, 5 per cent, 10 per cent significant levels, respectively. Robust standard errors are in parentheses.

Source: Same as Table 6.1.

Table 6.8

Gravity Model Regression Results

(i=30 OECD Countries; j=New Zealand)

Variable	*Dep. Var. ln (FDIij)*		*Dep. Var. ln (FDIij/GDPj)*	
	Random Effect	*IV*	*Random Effect*	*IV*
$\ln(FDI_{iASEAN5})$	0.0105 (0.03)	0.1968 *** (1.06)		
$\ln(FDI_{iASEAN5}/GDP_{ASEAN5})$			0.2164 *** (0.08)	0.8440 *** (0.10)
$\ln GDP_i$	-0.0255 * (0.01)	-0.0283 (0.09)	-0.0189 * (0.01)	-0.0723 *** (0.02)
$\ln GDP_j$	0.0478 (0.11)	-0.0159 (0.30)	-0.9849 *** (0.10)	-1.0040 *** (0.14)
$\ln GDPPC_i$	-0.0334 ** (0.02)	-0.0414 (0.08)	-0.0336 ** (0.01)	-0.0854 ** (0.04)
$\ln GDPPC_j$	-2.1167 *** (0.22)	-2.0473 *** (0.48)	-1.4167 *** (0.26)	0.7063 * (0.43)
ln*Dist*	0.0013 (0.04)	0.0415 (0.22)	0.0561 * (0.03)	0.2296 *** (0.07)
Landl	-0.0956 *** (0.03)	-0.1020 (0.17)	-0.0789 *** (0.02)	-0.1507 ** (0.07)
Constant	44.4560 *** (2.33)	40.9630 ** (20.03)	42.5528 *** (3.15)	22.5448 *** (4.78)
R^2	0.5174	0.4981	0.7795	0.5558
No. of Obs.	230	230	230	230

Notes: ***, **, * denote 1 per cent, 5 per cent, 10 per cent significant levels, respectively. Robust standard errors are in parentheses.

Source: Same as Table 6.1.

References

Anderson, James E. (1979). "A Theoretical Foundation for the Gravity Equation", *American Economic Review*, Vol. 69: 106-16.

Eichengreen, Barry and Hui Tong (2005). "Is China's FDI Coming at the Expense of Other Countries?", *NBER Working Paper* No. 11335. Cambridge: National Bureau of Economic Research.

Frankel, J., E. Stein and S. Wei (1995). "Trading Blocs and the Americas: The Natural, the Unnatural, and the Super-Natural", *Journal of Development Economics*, Vol. 47 (1): 61-95 (June).

Rose, Andrew (2005). "Which International Institutions Promote International Trade?", *Review of International Economics*, Vol. 13: 682-98.

Sudsawasd, Sasatra and Santi Chaisrisawatsuk (2005). "Does the Rising of China and India Crowd Out Trade and Foreign Direct Investments in Thailand?", Paper presented at the 30th Annual Conference of FAEA on *China and India: Challenges and Opportunities for ASEAN*. 24-25, November. Philippines.

Sudsawasd, Sasatra and Prasopchoke Mongsawad (2005). "On Rationale of Free Trade Agreements: The Case of ASEAN-5", Paper presented at the *Singapore Economic Review Conference 2005*. 4-6 August. Singapore.

www.aseansec.org

www.dtn.moc.go.th

www.mfa.go.th

www.asean-bac.org

7

Correcting Global Imbalances

Role of Regional Cooperation in Asia

RAMGOPAL AGARWALA and RAJIV KUMAR

Stellar Performance of Asia Despite Lack of Institutionalised Regional Cooperation Programmes

Some forty years ago, Nobel Laureate Gunnar Myrdal, in his monumental work, *The Asian Drama,* examined the prospects of Asia replicating the industrialisation experience of the West. Despite his deep empathy for Asia he concluded that because of various economic, social, cultural and political factors Asia was unlikely to achieve the western style growth rates of 3-4 per cent per year over a sustained period. Similar sentiments were expressed by many other economists and were the standard fare of the World Bank's country economic reports for Asia in the 1950s and early 1960s. History, however, had some surprises in store. Japan was the first to demonstrate that an Asian country can not only achieve but also surpass growth rates achieved by the West. By achieving double digit GDP (gross domestic product) growth rates during the 1960s, Japan created a new record in the annals of economic development. Although the growth rate slowed down in the 1970s the annual average growth rate over the 20-year period (1960-1980) was more than 7 per cent per year. Several other Asian countries—South Korea, Taiwan (China), Hong Kong, Singapore (often called the Asian Tigers)—followed soon to replicate the Japanese performance. Seven per cent annual GDP growth rate (a doubling of the GDP in one decade) became the benchmark during the 1970s and the 1980s in East Asia, including South East Asia. Then, from the 1980s onwards, China began to spring some more surprises. Several of its eastern provinces that were more than double the size (in terms of population) of the Asian Tigers began to grow at nearly double the growth rates achieved by the latter. The overall growth rate for this large country was over 9 per cent per annum for two decades after 1980, nearly quadrupling per capita incomes. China's achievement in poverty reduction and sustained growth since 1978 has been monumental and historically unprecedented.

South Asia, which for many decades seemed caught in the low growth rate trap has now moved close to the East Asian standard of 7 per cent annual growth and seems poised to move towards even higher growth rates in the coming decades. While India, which dominates any South Asian averages, has grown at nearly 7 per cent since beginning of the twenty-first century, Pakistan and Sri Lanka, the two other relatively large economies in the region have achieved growth rates of 5 per cent and 3 per cent, respectively, since 2001. These are indeed impressive performances and perhaps represent a new growth trajectory for South Asia in the coming years.

For all these high-performing economies, expansion of trade, in particular, growth of manufactured exports, played a crucial role in increasing productivity and sustaining rapid growth. Exports grew at a significantly faster rate than GDP in these economies throughout this period. The seminal pieces of work by, among others Anne Krueger pointed out how the process of getting into global markets creates special incentives and opportunities for improving quality and productivity.[1] Export promotion along with competitive markets and macroeconomic stability became standard tools recommended for accelerated and sustained growth.

Interestingly enough, even though development literature was replete with calls for promoting a trading bloc for accelerated growth in developing countries (often using the European Common Market as a model), preferential trading agreements (PTAs) played little or no role in Asia's rise. None of the high achievers—Japan, Korea, Taiwan, Singapore, Hong Kong and, most recently, China—was a member of any PTA. Rapidly growing exports to extra-regional partners were the dominant component of total exports *vis-a-vis* intra-regional trade. Even while intra-firm trade has gained recent importance in regional trade,

1. Krueger, 1978.

a significant part of this intra-firm/regional trade that arises from global production networks is dependent on extra-regional trade.

One major experiment in PTAs in Asia has been the ASEAN. However, the share of intra-regional trade in ASEAN has not registered any significant increase over time. The intra-regional trade ratio for ASEAN increased from 16.0 per cent in 1980 to 16.9 per cent in 1990 and to 21.2 per cent in 1995. This can be compared to intra-regional trade in the European Union (EU) (pre-expansion ratio of 65 per cent in 2002). During the second half of the 1990s efforts were made to accelerate regional integration through the formation of the AFTA (ASEAN Free Trade Area) in 1992 and an agreement for fast track trade liberalisation was made following the financial crisis of 1997. Yet, in 2004, the intra-regional trade ratio was only 22.4 per cent.[2] If trade and other programmes of regional cooperation in ASEAN were supposed to accelerate growth, the results are not evident. In fact, since 1992, ASEAN-5 has become the slowest growing subregion of Asia in terms of GDP growth rate (4.3 per cent per annum during 1992-2003) and exports (7.9 per cent per annum during 1992-2003). In 2004, with 8 per cent of GDP of Asia broadly defined (including East Asia, South Asia, Central Asia and West Asia), ASEAN certainly does not appear to be 'Middle Kingdom' for Asian cooperation.

In the light of these two facts, namely, rapid and sustained Asian economic growth without PTAs since the 1960s and the relatively modest performance of ASEAN—the one subregional PTA experiment in Asia—the question arises as to why one should bother with PTAs/FTAs in Asia. Participating in global trade that may be expected to grow as demonstrated in the past could provide the needed impetus for sustained growth and the case for PTAs in Asia would indeed be weak.

However, some recent developments in the global economy will not allow Asian economies to stick to business as usual. The United States is now suffering from unsustainable imbalances and there is

2. This is in line with the experience of most other PTAs in developing economies. See Schiff, Maurice and L. Alan Winters (2003). *Regionalism and Development*. New York: Oxford University Press.

now an urgent need to reduce Asia's reliance on exports to the United States and increase its imports from that country. This will contribute to the phased and manageable correction of the US imbalances and prevent an avoidable shock for the global economy. Given the size of US trade deficits, this demand switching has to take place on a large scale. And, given the current underutilisation of capacity in some of the major economies of Asia such as Japan, it is essential that such demand switching be accompanied by demand augmentation through open and market-oriented trading and financial systems that have served Asia well, without resorting to controls and protectionism either in Asia or in the United States. It is our contention that these new developments have created a need for developing a whole new paradigm for regional trade and economic cooperation in Asia which will help to sustain growth in Asia and at the same time reduce global economic imbalances. The key elements of our thesis are as follows:

First, in view of the enormity of the task involved, all of Asia (not only East Asia but also South, Central and West Asia) as well as Russia, Australia and New Zealand have to be involved in this programme for enhancing regional economic cooperation that covers trade, financial and investment flows. Thus, the definition or geographical coverage under Asia in our proposal is much wider than in earlier regional cooperation programmes.

Second, we would argue that open regionalism, as originally propounded by the Asia Pacific Economic Cooperation (APEC), provides the best framework for such enhanced trade cooperation with tariffs on a most favoured nation (MFN) basis and regional cooperation focusing on trade facilitation and non-discriminatory but trade-switching exchange rate policy.

Third, regional cooperation can help reduce global imbalances by promoting public investment in Asian regional infrastructure. Such increased investment in the region can facilitate trade and investment within the region and, by reducing the resources available for funding deficits, provide the necessary signal and push to the United States to reduce its imports and increase its exports.

The New Environment Created by Unsustainable Current Account Deficits of the US

Since the 1990s the United States has been running current account deficits which, in recent years, have assumed alarming proportions. And despite all the talk of reducing global imbalances, the US deficits keep on increasing. In 2005, these deficits increased to US$ 804.9 billion from US$ 668.1 billion in 2004. As a share of US GDP, the current account deficit rose to 6.4 per cent in 2005 from 5.7 per cent in 2004. By 2004, the foreign liabilities of the United States had already exceeded the foreign assets by US$ 2.5 trillion, which was more than the gross debt outstanding of all developing countries. Even though there are some who believe that the United States can manage such imbalances for the foreseeable future, the majority of analysts and policymakers believe that these imbalances are unsustainable and there are serious risks of disorderly correction of these imbalances with severe adverse consequences for the United States and the rest of the world.[3]

It is true that despite such alarm bells being sounded by many economists for the last few years, the United States continues to run large and growing current account deficits with no obvious immediate risks either to its own or to the world economy. However, this kind of prolongation is not atypical for 'bubbles' and the risks inherent in the current situation have been well articulated by Larry Summers (2006):

> To be sure the United States should be viewed differently from an emerging market and so there has been a certain amount of complacent commentary—commentary that has gained in strength as the US current account deficit has continued without evident ill effect. In general, my view thinking about past experience with tech stocks in the United States or with the Japanese stock market or with a range of emerging market situations is that the moment of maximum risk comes precisely when those concerned about sustainability lose confidence in their views as their warnings prove to have been premature and when rationalisations come to the forefront.

3. Reference to webpage on global imbalances.

Some standard recipes for reducing these imbalances have been proposed in the literature, namely, exchange rate changes in China, structural reforms in Japan, reflation in the EU and austerity in the US. However, even though World Bank/International Monetary Fund reports prescribe these medicines, the results of the analysis presented in the reports show only modest improvements in global imbalances as a result of applying these medicines. For example, the IMF (2005b), concludes that even in a benign adjustment scenario, US current account deficit will declinc to about 3.5 per cent of GDP by 2010 and to 3 per cent of GDP in the long run, with the US net foreign liabilities eventually stabilising at about 70 per cent of GDP. This would still be a high level of indebtedness even by the standards of highly indebted developing countries.

Clearly, some bolder programmes of reform are needed if the US current account deficits are to be reduced. These deficits reflect decline in savings rate in the United States, on the one hand, and decline in investment rates in many emerging economies of Asia, on the other. Corrective action is needed on both these counts. In order to reduce the propensity for high consumption, the United States needs to face a harder external budget constraint and accept lower real income through devaluation of the dollar and the consequent terms of trade effect. The current dollar reserve system prevents an effective devaluation of the dollar and creates a soft external budget constraint for the United States. This must give way to a multipolar foreign exchange reserve system if the US problem of excess consumption is to be tackled. However, if the US savings rate is increased without any increase in demand in the rest of the world, there would be a risk of serious recession in the world economy. Thus simultaneous action is needed to increase demand in Asia and we would argue that the immediate areas of action lie in increasing public investments in infrastructure (both regional and domestic) which would in turn increase private investment and consumption.

Afraid of competition from Asian exports, many countries in Europe and America are calling for reducing Asia's reliance on exports (in the new language, 'addiction' to exports) and for increasing 'domestic demand'. For example, the Treasury Secretary, John Snow, told the

International Monetary and Financial Committee (IMFC)—on 24 September, 2005 that what is 'necessary for smooth global adjustment is a shift from export-led to domestic demand-led growth'. In view of the merits of export-orientation as noted above, it would be a mistake for Asia to move away from exports *per se*. The way to reconcile the need to reduce exports from Asia to the United States and the need to keep up export orientation is to redirect Asia's exports from the United States to Asia. In other words, there should be a shift to 'domestic demand' on a regional basis but not on a country basis.

The strategy proposed in this paper has three components:

- regional trade facilitation measures to increase intra-regional trade;
- concerted exchange rate policy in Asia for facilitating devaluation of the US dollar in relation to Asian currencies; and
- increased infrastructure investment to cure 'investment drought' and strengthen regional domestic demands in Asia.

Trade Facilitation Activities (TFAs) rather than Free Trade Areas (FTAs)

Despite the low payoffs in terms of trade and income from the PTAs in Asia and other developing countries there has been, in recent years, a great surge in PTAs worldwide, including Asia. The pattern commonly followed is the one of 'hub and spokes' where large economies such as the United States, Japan and China are negotiating bilateral deals with smaller economies. This pattern allows focus on areas of mutual interest and avoids issues such as agricultural protection and subsidies which are becoming contentious at, the multilateral level. Among the FTAs that have been signed or are under active negotiation are those of Singapore-Japan, Singapore-US, Singapore-Australia, Singapore-India, Japan-Korea, Japan-Mexico, Japan-ASEAN, Japan-Korea-China, China-ASEAN, China-India, ASEAN-US, ASEAN-Korea, India-Sri Lanka, India-Thailand, India-ASEAN and Japan-ASEAN.

The fact of this surge in FTAs deserves serious attention and analysis but the surge by itself is no guarantee of its being the right policy. After all, there was an even greater surge for import-substitution policies and planning in developing countries in the 1950s and the 1960s which, in retrospect, turned out to be misguided. The benefits of FTAs have to be demonstrated by concrete analysis and not just presumed because of their popularity. Analysis done, among others, by the World Bank, 2005 shows much lower gains from trade liberalisation on bilateral and regional basis than on multilateral basis. In fact the report highlights a 'fallacy of composition' argument which may help understand the interest of many developing countries in signing FTAs with larger developed countries. The modelling exercise done for the report shows that:

> Each developing country could raise its real incomes by individually signing bilateral agreements with the Quad countries [United States, EU, Canada and Japan]; and in some cases they would raise their real incomes more than they would through multilateral accords. But these gains disappear if all developing countries were to sign such agreements. In fact, all developing countries would lose relative to a multilateral agreement and even relative to the baseline.

It has been pointed out by the World Bank 'Rules of Origin in Free Trade Agreements', 2003 and others that the complicated rules of origin in FTAs increase costs of transaction of trade and may also create vested interests in protecting particular sectors. This will hamper subsequent multilateral liberalisation. So we strongly support the continuation and strengthening of the multilateral trading regime as enshrined in the WTO and hope that all Asian governments will contribute to the success of the Doha Round by sinking their differences and agreeing to a lower level of ambition. This will be a move in the direction of creating a level playing field in agriculture, which has now emerged as the most insurmountable hurdle to the successful conclusion of the Round.

While relying on the multilateral liberalisation framework for liberalisation of tariffs, regional trade cooperation agreements could more usefully focus on reducing transaction costs of trade which still remains high in Asia. The World Bank report on trade, regionalism and development has highlighted that these costs of trade among developing countries could be tax equivalent of 30-105 per cent, depending on the sector.[4] Among these costs are:

- transport costs, both direct (freight and insurance) and indirect (inventory costs);
- costs incurred when crossing a border due to documentation, delays and bribes to corrupt officials;
- compliance with national product standards and technical regulations; and
- insurance against risk, especially credit risks and uncertainty associated with macroeconomic instability and lack of effective institutions.

One advantage of implementing measures to address the above-mentioned transaction costs is that they can be adopted by two or more countries without necessarily requiring a region-wide agreement. These activities can be 'project-oriented' and the scope of cooperation can vary from project to project. This leads to what has been called 'variable geometry' in regional cooperation which may fit in well with the recent urge towards PTAs without bringing in the complications associated with tariff liberalisation on regional basis.

The scope for these measures can perhaps be illustrated with reference to the possible improvement in surface and air transport within Asia. Because of historical reasons the transport system in Asia has been geared to the 'hub and spokes' system with transportation between periphery and core being easier than between different parts of the periphery. There are many landlocked countries and remote regions of large countries which have become pockets of low income and high level of poverty partly because of high transport costs. Many of these regions were thriving economically when they were on the famed 'silk routes' of the past. Better surface transport can help revive these regions and subregions (covering not only geographic Asia but also Russia and other CIS countries). Not only will this accelerate growth in the region but will also contribute more than proportionately to poverty reduction. There have been many Pan-Asian road and

4. See also Roy (2005).

railway projects proposed, among others, by the United Nations Economic and Social Commission for Asia and the Pacific (UNESCAP). But they have not taken off because of lack of funds and proper institutional mechanism for implementing them. A determined regional infrastructure development programme can contribute massively to improving regional transport and increasing regional trade.

Similar opportunities for trade expansion lie in the improvement of trade in oil and gas in the region. The Ministerial Round Table (held in New Delhi in November 2005) on cooperation between North and Central Asian producers and principal Asian consumers, regarding stability, security and sustainability in the Asian hydrocarbon economy, highlighted the enormous scope for investments in exploration, development transmission of oil and gas resources of Asia and Russia and other Commonwealth of Independent States (CIS) countries. Here again, an institutional mechanism needs to be developed to activate investments which are likely to have a very high rate of return.

Concerted Exchange Rate Policy and Creation of an Asian Currency Unit

The need for devaluation of the dollar is readily accepted by the US authorities but they seem to be singling out one country (China) for that treatment. It is true that over the last 25 years of its development, China has devalued its currency by over 70 per cent in real effective terms and has gained tremendously in export competitiveness. Over time, as its labour productivity increases in relative terms, its real effective exchange rate should also increase, as has been the case with Japan and South Korea. However, the Chinese authorities are rightly resistant of the high-handed pressures from the US for revaluation of their currency. As Ronald McKinnon, Professor of International Economics at Stanford University, has argued, the Chinese may well be afraid of repeating the Japanese experience on revaluation under pressure. In the case of Japan, when revaluation of the yen was, as predicted by most analysts, unable to cure the US trade deficits in the early 1980s, they were pressured into repeated revaluations which did little to cure the US trade deficits but succeeded in pushing the Japanese economy into prolonged stagnation. It has been shown by a number of economists that revaluation of the Chinese yuan by itself will do little to cure the trade deficits of the US. If China starts yielding to the US pressure on unilateral revaluation, it may be blamed for not doing enough and be pushed into the Japanese scenario of repeated revaluations and a possible economic stagnation.

For greater impact on the US trade deficits and for minimising intra-Asian trade distortions, a concerted exchange rate management policy in Asia may be called for. In recent years, exchange rates in most Asian countries have gone through major gyrations not only in relation to the US dollar and the Euro but also among themselves. Such exchange rate instabilities create uncertainties which cannot be conducive to trade and investment. The problem can perhaps be best illustrated with reference to the exchange rate between the Yen and the Yuan. The bilateral exchange rate between these two has fluctuated widely over the last 10 years (with year to year change often more than 10 per cent up or down) but around a trend toward depreciation of the Japanese yen in relation to the Chinese yuan as well as the US dollar (Table 7.1).

Table 7.1

Bilateral Exchange Rates between Japan and China

	Yen Per Dollar (Year Average)	*Chinese Yuan Per Dollar (Year Average)*	*Yen per Yuan (Year Average)*	*Per cent change in Yen-Yuan Rate*
1994	102.21	8.62	11.9	
1995	94.06	8.35	11.3	-5
1996	108.78	8.31	13.1	16
1997	120.99	8.29	14.6	11
1998	130.91	8.28	15.8	8
1999	113.91	8.28	13.7	-13
2000	107.77	8.28	13.0	-5
2001	121.53	8.28	14.7	13
2002	125.39	8.28	15.1	3
2003	115.93	8.28	14.0	-7
2004	108.19	8.28	13.1	-7
2005	110.22	8.20	13.4	3

Source: IMF (2006).

At present it is widely believed that the equilibrium exchange rate for the yen could be lower than the current rate of about 117 per US dollar. However, with the current exchange rate policy of China, a substantial appreciation of the Yen will reduce the competitiveness of the Japanese economy *vis-à-vis* China in a situation when Japan is already suffering from trade deficits with China. A simultaneous revaluation of both the currencies may be much more acceptable to Japan. Now is the time to examine how the Asian economies, which are experiencing a relatively rapid increase in labour productivity and a healthy balance of payments position, can revalue their currencies in relation to the US dollar in a concerted manner. Such revaluations will not be done under pressure and will take into account the value of currencies not only in relation to the US dollar but also amongst the Asian countries themselves.

Any programme of devaluation of the dollar, however, faces the problem created by the limited number of currencies with reserve currency status. At present more than 90 per cent of the official foreign exchange reserves (2.5 trillion SDRs in end 2004) are held in US dollar (66 per cent) and Euro (25 per cent). Thus a switching out of the US dollar often means switching into the Euro and the consequent revaluation of the Euro. As shown by recent experience, such large revaluation of the Euro may not be conducive to the health of European economies and the European authorities may well be constrained to recycle their dollar inflows back to dollar to keep their currency in a comfortable zone. This problem can be alleviated if there is at least one more reserve currency such as an Asian currency unit. A common currency for Asia may not be feasible in the foreseeable future but a parallel currency along the lines of what was envisaged with IMF's SDR (but was not allowed to be implemented by the powers that be) is eminently feasible. And as a step towards such currency an Asian Currency Unit (ACU) as a unit of account can be launched almost immediately. If price quotations start being made in ACU they would reduce fluctuations of terms of trade and in terms of capital movements among Asian countries which in turn can be expected to contribute to increased intra-regional trade and investment. And as Asian currencies become linked to the ACU, concerted adjustments in Asian exchange rates would become easier. The Asian Development Bank (ADB) has taken the first step by starting a statistical exercise to prepare a composite of some Asian currencies. Unfortunately, at present this basket seems to include only the currencies of the ASEAN+3 countries. If the ACU is to provide a significant alternative reserve asset, it must be backed by economic strength, perhaps comparable to those of the United States and the EU. Similarly, to maximise the benefits of intra-regional trade and investment through relative stability of intra-regional exchange rates in real terms, the coverage of the currency must be such so as to maximise the complementarities of Asian economies in trade and investment. From both these angles, it makes sense to make the ACU inclusive of all the major Asian economies in East Asia, South Asia and West Asia as well as Russia and other CIS countries. It will also be helpful to include currencies of Australia and New Zealand in this basket in so far as these countries have a well-functioning currency market and a mature financial system. Even as a unit of account, the ACU will get a strong start if oil-producing countries of the region start quoting oil price in the ACU.

A Trillion Dollar Ten-year Programme of Investment Boost in the Region

The IMF has identified 'investment drought' in Asia as a major factor behind global imbalances.

> Investment rates in emerging Asia excluding China, which had increased markedly in the years before the Asian crisis, collapsed sharply during the crisis (by 8 percentage points of GDP between 1996 and 1998). Investment rates have remained depressed since the crisis, having risen by only 2 percentage points of GDP from 1998 levels....Both public and private investment declined, and are each still below pre-crisis levels. Domestically-financed investment has experienced the sharpest decline; after dipping slightly, FDI has returned to pre-crisis levels. These developments point to the emergence of an 'investment drought', rather than a 'saving glut' in emerging Asia excluding China (IMF, 2005a).

The IMF believes that the solution lies in stimulating private investment and warns against reliance on public investment.[5] On this it may be wrong on both counts: the potential of private investment *per se* may not be high enough to cure the investment drought and the risks of public investment may not be as great as the IMF believes.

The private sector on its own is inadequate for curing the investment drought. In order to realise this, all we need to do is to look at the experience of Asia over the last 10 years beginning 1997 specially in the ASEAN region and Central Asia. Structural reforms have been going on in Central Asia and South East Asia for nearly a decade; but private investment remains sluggish. In the case of Central Asia it can be clearly seen that the IMF's expectations in private investment and productivity arising from structural reforms has simply not been borne out.

An alternative approach is to view public and private investment as complementary and this is supported by, among others, the experience of China. In China public investment, including infrastructure investments, have been high and these presumably helped to attract private investments from both domestic and foreign sources.

The view of synergy between public and private investment is also supported by investment climate surveys. Business climate studies of the World Bank typically show inadequate infrastructure as a constraint on private investment. Also, experience in India and elsewhere has demonstrated that in infrastructure externalities are important and the private sector alone cannot make the necessary investment.

In India, complementarity of private and public sector investment is being accepted and Public-Private-Partnership (PPP) is emerging as the tool of choice for encouraging infrastructure investments. PPP offers advantages in terms of cost saving, access to specialised expertise and proprietary technology and sharing of risks with the private sector. To support PPP in infrastructure, the Government of India has taken two major initiatives: (a) provision of viability gap

---

5. In the 2006 spring meetings of IMF, a small beginning has been made in recognising the role of infrastructure investment in surplus countries to the extent that there were calls for "increasing investment in energy-related infrastructure in oil-producing countries."

funding, and (b) setting up of a Special Purpose Vehicle (SPV)—India Infrastructure Finance Company Limited (IIFCL)—to meet the long-term financing requirements of potential investors. The viability gap funding will normally be in the form of a capital grant at the stage of project construction, not exceeding 20 per cent of the total project cost. The IIFCL will finance up to 20 per cent of the project cost either by direct lending to eligible projects or by refinance to banks and financial institutions for loans with 10 or more years. The rate of interest charged by the IIFCL shall be such as to cover all fund costs including guarantee fee as well as administrative costs.

The approach taken by India for supporting infrastructure development may be considered for upscaling at the regional level. An Asian Infrastructure Bank along the lines of the IIFCL may be set up to mobilise funds from countries with 'excess' foreign exchange reserves and to support projects in the PPP mode. Viability gap funding may also be required with contributions from more developed countries in Asia.

The IMF (2005a) has argued against the use of the PPP mode for increasing infrastructure investments and also against the accumulation of foreign exchange reserves for financing public investment. According to the IMF:

> The benefits of PPPs should not be oversold, in particular, their ability to provide infrastructure without affecting the government's balance sheet. PPPs can generate fiscal liabilities regardless of whether the financing of the asset entails gross borrowing by the government. As such, transparent reporting of the capital value of all PPPs and of the uncontingent and contingent liabilities associated with these projects is essential. Otherwise, PPPs may become an easy tool to bypass spending controls and to give the illusion of a larger fiscal envelope.

And also:

> Reserve-financed public investment is essentially just central bank credit to government, where the debt is in the form of liabilities issued by the central bank when purchasing the foreign reserves. This proposal also entails the risk that public investment decisions will take place outside the usual vetting framework. Potential transparency and governance problems would argue for keeping spending on such

projects in the budget, rather than creating a separate entity capitalised by excess reserves. Last, but not least, financing infrastructure through the use of reserves can impinge on the independence of the monetary authority.

In our view, the arguments of the IMF are somewhat misplaced. The IMF believes that public investments are not productive enough to justify public borrowing. However, there is growing evidence in Asia that public investment to develop infrastructure can have high payoffs in terms of direct and indirect economic benefits to the economy and the public exchequer. As in the case of any private company, the debt position of the government should be judged in relation to its assets and if infrastructure investments along with the land assets acquired during the process more than offset the increase in debt, the net indebtedness need not increase. The issues of transparency and governance are economy-wide issues and not specifically about infrastructure financing. In fact, because of the high profile nature of these investments, they are under vetting more fully than what is typically provided in budgeted expenditure. As regards monetary authorities, their independence has to be seen in the context of the needs and priorities of the society of which they are a part and, if additional infrastructure investment is good for the country, monetary authorities themselves should come forward to facilitate the funding of such investments.

If an Asian Infrastructure Bank is set up, it can serve the infrastructure investment needs of Asia. Pending an in-depth assessment of regional infrastructure investment needs, it appears that infrastructure in Asia can easily absorb more than US$ 100 billion additional annual investment over the next 10 years. There are of course plenty of regional funds waiting for profitable investment opportunities. An AIB can help in designing, financing and implementing these regional investment programmes. An immediate beginning can be made by setting up regional entities for implementing some high quality investment programmes such as gas and oil pipelines, IT, and highways and railways within Asia. The ADB, according to its Charter, would have been the right agency for leading the process but its current structure makes it difficult for it to respond to demands quickly and without political interference. In any case, the magnitude of the additional investments required is much beyond the current financing capacity of the ADB and there is need for an Asian Infrastructure Bank (perhaps modelled on the European Investment Bank) which will not suffer from the constraints of the ADB and will help redirect part of Asia's massive foreign exchange reserves to Asian infrastructure.

Beginning with an investment of, say, US$ 50 billion, these additional public and private investments could perhaps rise to some US$ 150 billion over a 10-year period. Subject to the results of the modelling exercise, one can surmise that through multiplier and accelerator effects, these investments could over time create additional demand of over US$ 300 billion per year, thus providing an alternative source of demand for a substantial part of the US current account gap (currently over US$ 800 billion). As mentioned earlier, this process of using more of Asian reserves in Asia will harden the external budget constraint on the United States and help improve its saving performance.

Conclusion: An Opportunity for Win-Win Solution for Asia and the Rest of the World

For developing Asia (except China) these additional investments could easily amount to 5-10 per cent of GDP and they can be expected to add 1-2 percentage points of additional growth. With greater connectivity among Asian countries, the landlocked countries and the landlocked regions of the large countries can become 'land-linked' and share more fully in the rising prosperity of the continent; thus increasing the gains in poverty reduction.

Japan may be able to utilise its excess capacity in capital goods industries better and resume a growth rate similar to that of other OECD (Organization for Economic Cooperation and Development) countries. The construction industry in particular is suffering from excess capacity and increased infrastructure investment in Asia can give a boost to this important industry in Japan.

Barry Eichengreen, Professor of Economics and Political Science in the University of California[6] and others have argued that from the

6. Eichengreen, 2005.

economic point of view Asia satisfies conditions for rapid financial and economic integration but the process is constrained by political factors. There are indeed many ongoing political differences amongst major economic players in Asia. But lack of support from the global intellectual and political leader, namely, the United States, may have been the crucial stumbling block to regional cooperation in Asia. As seen in the case of regional trade agreements, a change of opinion in the United States can make a major difference to the prevailing opinion in Asia and elsewhere. If the United States begins to see regional cooperation in Asia as an opportunity for correcting its current account imbalances, and thus facilitate the redressal of global imbalances, it can give a big boost to regional cooperation in Asia. Asia would then be able to play a stronger role in sustaining global economic growth which would bring down global poverty levels.

References

Brenton, Paul (2003). *Rules of Origin in Free Trade Agreements*, Trade Note 4, World Bank, The World BankGroup. *www.worldbank.org*. International Trade Department. *http://siteresources.worldbank.org/INTRANETTRADE/Resources/TradeNote4.pdf*

Eichengreen, Barry (2005). "Real and Pseudo Preconditions for an Asian Monetary Union", in *Asian Economic Cooperation and Integration: Progress, Prospects and Challenges*. Manila Philippines: Asian Development Bank.

Krueger, Anne O. (1978). "Foreign Trade Regimes and Economic Development: Liberalisation Attempts and Consequences." New York: NBER.

Roy, Jayanta (2005). "South Asian Regional Trade Agreements: Perspectives, Issues and Options", paper presented at the International Trade Round Table, *The WTO at 10 Years—The Regional Challenge to Multilateralism*, 27 June, Brussels.

Schiff, Maurice and Alan Winters (2003). *Regionalism and Development*. New York: Oxford University Press.

Summers, Lawrence H. (2006). "Reflections of Global Account Imbalances and Emerging Markets Reserve Accumulation", *L.K. Jha Memorial Lecture*, Mumbai: RBI, 24 March.

The International Monetary Fund (2006). *International Financial Statistics Yearbook*. Washington DC.

The International Monetary Fund (2005a). Asia and Pacific Department, *Asia-Pacific Regional Outlook*. *www.imf.org/Pubs/FT/weo/2005/02/index.htm*

———. (2005b). *World Economic Outlook: Building Institutions www.imf.org/Pubs/FT/weo/2005/02/index.htm*. Washington DC.

The World Bank (2003). *Rules of Origin in Free Trade Agreements*. Washington DC.

———. (2004). *Global Economic Prospects 2005: Trade, Regionalism and Development*. Washington DC.

Nouriel Roubini's Blog:*www.rgemonitor.com/blog/roubini*

Index

Symbols

A

D

E

F

G

H

L

M

N

O

P

Q

R

U

V

W

Y